Where Angels Fear

SHY KEENAN is an awarded Victims' Advocate who founded Phoenix Survivors to campaign for better child protection and justice, victims' services and offender management. Her work has been recognised by the British government as a crucial part of the battle to protect children. She lives with her family in the countryside.

SARA PAYNE won the hearts of the country when she appealed for the return of her missing daughter Sarah. The whole nation grieved when Sarah's body was found. She works to prevent a similar tragedy occurring again and lives with her family. She was awarded an MBE earlier this year, and has been appointed Victims' Champion.

In 2008, both Shy and Sara were awarded Women of the Year for their work together as the Phoenix Chief Advocates.

Where Angels Fear

Shy Keenan
and
Sara Payne, MBE

HODDER

Publisher's Note
Names and locations have been changed throughout
in order to protect the identities of individuals

First published in Great Britain in 2009 by Hodder & Stoughton
An Hachette UK company

First published in paperback in 2010

2

A CIP catalogue record for this title is available from the British Library.

ISBN 978 0 340 93747 1

Typeset in Monotype Sabon by Ellipsis Books Limited, Glasgow

Printed and bound in the UK by CPI Mackays, Chatham ME5 8TD

Hodder & Stoughton policy is to use papers that are natural,
renewable and recyclable products and made from wood grown in
sustainable forests. The logging and manufacturing processes are expected
to conform to the environmental regulations of the country of origin.

Hodder & Stoughton Ltd
338 Euston Road
London NW1 3BH

www.hodder.co.uk

We dedicate this book to every Phoenix; don't waste your life on hate and fear, the greatest revenge is to survive and survive well.

Acknowledgements

First and foremost we would like to thank our families and loved ones; you keep the lights on in our darkest times, and because of you we love and feel loved.

Special thanks go to all those who have helped us write and publish this book. To all those who allowed us to tell their stories and shared their pain with us, in the hope that one day things will change for the better. And finally, to all of those people who have helped us, educated us and supported us; you have helped to restore our faith in 'good' and we both know we would be nothing without you. Thank you.

Contents

Foreword   1

Introduction   5

Part One
Rising from the Ashes   11

Part Two
Survivors   63

Part Three
The Retreat   217

Part Four
Rebuilding the Dam   295

Epilogue   305

Foreword

When Shy and I began work on this book, we swiftly worked out that of the two of us, she was better suited to actually sitting down and writing it, so it's her voice you'll hear from here on. It's only right that she should be the main storyteller, because this book tells the story of our work helping the victims of paedophiles as a Phoenix – first as Phoenix Survivors, then as the Phoenix Chief Advocates. And Shy *is* Phoenix. She founded Phoenix. She started it from nothing, funded it and, for a while, ran it single-handedly – until I came on board and we formed a team based not only on a shared set of values and a common goal, but also on friendship.

When I joined, I soon realised that Shy was the heart and soul of Phoenix. She was not just loved and relied upon, but she was also a trusted friend to many people. Ask anyone who has worked with her and they will tell you that she has touched their life, either privately or professionally. Some will tell you that she has saved their life, but all will say that she is what inspires them to survive, to fight back, to work harder, to do better.

She's had to make many sacrifices for it. To fund Phoenix and keep it going, she's used her victim-compensation money, the proceeds from her first book, *Broken*, and she's even sold valuable possessions. She's never minded doing it; she'd tell you herself that she chooses to do what she does.

As you're about to discover, however, the fight to keep Phoenix going has not been without its casualties. Because as much as this is the story of our work with the victims of child sex abuse and our fight against the abusers, it's also the story of our fight to give victims a fairer deal and a louder voice.

Separately, we both bring skills to the table in our work, but when we work together, something unique happens. We have had so many incredible ups and downs, and so much has happened since we came to work together. The stories we cover in the book are really just the tip of the iceberg.

There are some very dark, sad things about our work, but we have each other and our friendship, which helps us deal with whatever comes our way, good or bad. Yes, our work is hard and often horrible, but we do get to do something about it: we get a chance to change some of those horrible things for the better, and these days we succeed more than we fail.

Shy and I are not just colleagues; she is one of my dearest friends. I've seen Shy pick up a victim from the depths of absolute darkness and show them how to reach the light; it is quite something to witness. She has the biggest heart of anyone I know and one of the kindest of natures. She is massively protective of those she loves and cares for, and when she loves and cares about you, you know it. Shy is loyal, dependable and as fiercely stubborn as I am, and when she fights for others, she's fearless. I have learned so much from her. She has taught me to be proud of my strengths and to respect my weaknesses.

Shy has a very serious side, especially when it comes to work, but she can also have me in absolute fits, tears of laughter, flat on the floor. She is truly one in a million. You can fall into her friendship and know that no matter what she will catch you. I would trust her with my life. She showed me how to trust again and I will always love her for that.

This is her story, but it's also our story. We do our work as Phoenix with hope, humour and heart, and we've written the book with the same guiding principles. Thank you for reading and for giving us your time. In return I can only promise that together we'll continue to go where most angels fear to tread.

Sara Payne, MBE, 2009

Introduction

It took all kinds of horror to bring Sara and me together; ours is a friendship forged from the loss of innocence. In my case, my own: first I was emotionally and physically abused by my mother, then emotionally, physically and sexually abused by my stepfather, Stanley Claridge, and others. In Sara's case it was the innocence of a nation, when her daughter Sarah was kidnapped and killed by a paedophile, Roy Whiting, in 2000.

You no doubt remember. Sarah was a sweet, happy eight-year-old who had been playing with her older brothers and younger sister on a beach at Kingston Gorse, near Littlehampton. Lee, Luke and their sister, Charlotte, had insisted they were fine to play without adult supervision, and the two lads were very responsible, so after much soul-searching, Sara, her husband Mike, and Mike's dad had agreed and the adults had continued their late-afternoon walk.

The kids had played in rock pools for a while but got bored and decided to run around in a nearby field instead. While there, Sarah had fallen over and, because she was hurt, decided to go back to her nanny's house (just a couple of hundred yards away). She darted off, her speed catching her brothers by surprise. At the same time, Charlotte was stung by nettles, arresting one of the boy's attention for a moment while the other ran after Sarah. When her brother next looked towards where Sarah had been running, she was gone.

The search began and it made the news. Next, Sara appeared on a TV press conference that was broadcast nationwide.

That's when I first saw her. At the time, I was staying in a hotel filming a *Newsnight* documentary called 'A Family Affair'. Imagine you're helping to make a documentary that will reveal your stepfather to be the head of a paedophile ring; it's going to blow your birth family apart. Imagine you're about to tell the world about things done to you from the age of three, that you were used as an orifice by paedophiles for a massive portion of your childhood. The process was taking a lot out of me. I was exhausted, nervous, worried for the future – the whole works. I was so nervous and frightened I was pacing the room and so flicked on the TV to keep me company and distract me.

It was then I saw Sara. The same Sara you saw: long, dark, unkempt hair, worry and fatigue sculpted into her face, eyes wide and beseeching. The sight of her brought my heart into my mouth and tears to my eyes. Whatever I was feeling, it paled in comparison to what she was going through, and this, remember, was before we knew the worst.

There was something else I felt too. Describing it is difficult, but it was as though there was some kind of emotional connection between us. I felt close to her, like we had a painful knowledge in common. Sara and her family were clearly in agony, but despite all that was happening to them, you could practically feel the strength emanating from her as she pleaded to the world to help her find her baby.

And guess what? Sometime later Sara would see me on telly too, and she'd have exactly the same feelings. Sitting in front of our respective TV screens, we both sort of said, 'All right, sweetheart, how are you doing?' We were each transmitting silent messages of support to each other as if to say, 'I'm here for you, girl.' You could say we met across a crowded television screen.

That was it for a while. In the meantime, some terrible things went down: Sarah's body was discovered, Roy Whiting was arrested, then came the trial. In my world, the police swooped on Claridge and friends, there were trials and convictions, and eventually I would start Phoenix Survivors, more of which later.

It was in 2003 that a friend at the *News of the World* put us in touch with each other. The paper had just awarded me the first ever Britain's Children's Champion Award and was also helping to promote the Sarah's Law campaign, headed up by Sara. Through that contact, we got in touch with each other and our friendship began.

We spoke on the phone, not much at first, once a month perhaps. We didn't see each other at all. I rarely go out anyway, thanks to my agrosociophobia, a legacy of the abuse. It means if I go outside, or try to do something outside my comfort zone, hyperhidrosis kicks in, which in my case is sweating from the back of my head. As a result, I tend to remain in environments in which I'm comfortable. If I go out, it's always a major event.

Gradually, we began gravitating towards each other

more and more. Monthly calls became fortnightly, then weekly. We spoke about how we were doing that day: like today's a good day; yesterday was a bad day; the day before that was a bad, black day. We talked about the news, current events, our day-to-day lives. Soon we were talking on an almost daily basis, sometimes for hours at a time. Slowly, almost without noticing, we became the best of friends.

Ours is a very modern friendship. We use phone, email and instant messaging. We both have webcams we use with a piece of software called Skype, so even though we rarely get together, we meet up over Skype, sometimes several times a day. That way, we can see and hear each other. It's almost always on, so we're in near-constant contact. In fact, we call it our 'virtual office' because even though we're not physically in the same room, we are face to face and we share all of the same facilities and resources. It enables us to work very closely together on everything we do.

And the work? Well, Sara and I have taken our friendship and built something with it. We are the Phoenix Chief Advocates. We advocate for the victims of paedophiles and for the families of children abducted and/or murdered by child molesters. We do it voluntarily. We do it because we have to.

As much as we may hate it, Claridge and Whiting were in some way responsible for bringing us together. We're not going to waste time mourning the fact that we couldn't have met under happier circumstances, though. Instead, we've got on with taking care of business – ensuring that Claridge and Whiting and others like them never go unchallenged. Never.

This book is the story of our work as Phoenixes. We will reveal what is happening in our country at this very moment, the terrible acts that human beings living in our community are committing right now. We'll also reveal the many injustices that allow them to continue. But it is far more than a catalogue of crime; it is the story of the extraordinary things that two ordinary women can achieve. Some of what we have to say is disturbing and shocking. Please read on, for while this is a story of cruelty and despair, it is also, ultimately, a story of hope.

Part One

Rising from the Ashes

I

The first seed of an idea for Phoenix Survivors began on a flight of steps in Liverpool. It began with my mascara streaked by tears, and a profound sense that, though some justice had at last been done, the world had turned its back on us. It began with reporters shouting, 'Shy!' and, 'How do you feel, Shy?'

A sharp, bright March evening in 2002 and I was stood outside Liverpool Crown Court, having come from the gallery and on to the steps of the courthouse. The *Newsnight* documentary I'd made had sparked Operation Phoenix, which in turn had led to the court case. Stanley, my stepfather, and two others had been jailed for their crimes. At last, after years of anguish, of abuse, of screaming for justice and my cries going ignored, I'd had my day in court.

After all those years of abuse, finally someone had listened to me. It had been a long wait. The abuse had begun when I was a baby. It had started with my mother, Jennifer, a bingo addict who neglected me by leaving me half-naked in my urine-soaked cot twenty-four hours a day. That was when she was with Fred, my real father. Compared to what was to come, however, those were the good times. After my mother split up with Fred, she married Stanley Claridge, who became my stepfather. He

was a liar and a violent former alcoholic. He was also a
paedophile. I first met him when I was aged about three
or four, when we went to visit him just prior to moving
into his house in Southall. That was the first time he
abused me – he pulled me on to his lap and I felt a sharp
pain in my bottom; when I tried to wriggle free, my mother
told me I had to be nice to my new daddy and sit still.
So I did.

After we'd moved in, the abuse began in earnest. My
mother was happy to let Stanley take care of me and my
sisters while she was out – and she was out a lot – so Stanley
had free rein. One of my earliest memories involves being
naked in a darkened room, a flash going off and the sound
of clicking. I know it now to be a camera, of course, but
then all I knew was that the flashing lights and clicking
sound meant that the pain down below would shortly begin
– that soon Stanley would be moving up and down on top
of me.

This went on for years. Stanley passed me around his
friends, who abused me, photographed me, filmed me,
beat me badly and even, on one particularly horrific occasion, left me for dead. They were, I would later discover,
a network of paedophiles. Every time I tried to speak out
about it, I was either branded a liar or accused of leading
the men on. I was taken away from Stanley's home and
placed into care on and off throughout my childhood,
but the abuse continued – this time by those employed to
care for me. So many times I tried to tell and was ignored,
or I told and was ignored. I became an adult and my voice
continued to be ignored. I sent the police a tape of Stanley
admitting what he'd done and *still* no action was taken.

Then it became clear that a new generation of victims was now at risk from Stanley and his friends. I knew I had to do something more extreme.

It was a last throw of the dice. I went to the media. With the help of Colm O'Gorman from the victim-support charity One in Four, I contacted *Newsnight*, who made a sixty-minute special called 'A Family Affair'. At last the authorities took action. Finally, I was believed. Arrests were made and I had my day in court.

And now, standing outside the court, I blinked away tears that refracted the world as if seen through diamonds. I tried to focus on the reporters, their faces splitting and distorting through my tears. Microphones were thrust towards my face, and questions were fired at me.

'Shy!'

'How do you feel, Shy?'

I was getting flashbacks, triggered by the blasts of camera flash. The flashing lights. The pain. Imagine a photograph that changes its image every second, playing out a sequence of horrifying childhood memories: you being raped, your mother beating you, a kettle of hot water scalding you, your baby sister crying out in pain, a sparse jail cell. Feelings of horror, revulsion, shame, fear and loneliness. Now imagine you are forced to look at those photographs several times a day, when you're chatting with friends, having a meal or watching telly. You try to look through those pictures, under them, around them, over them, anywhere except at them, but you can't. Then an evil projectionist in your head awakes and starts rolling the mini films that play in your mind. *Actually right in front of your eyes*. Complete with smells, sounds and feelings. You flick your head from side to side, trying to blink the images away.

This is how it is for me. Most of the time I manage to carry on as if the images aren't really there, but sometimes their intensity catches me by surprise, stops me dead in my tracks. I can be talking at a zillion words a second, which is about my normal rate, then suddenly . . . stop. The blinking starts, then the stammering, followed closely by the sweating. And I'll be taken back to a room in Southall . . .

That day, though, I was determined to blank out the images. I wasn't going to let any of that get in my way, not right there, on the steps outside Liverpool Crown Court. I'd come too far.

I had prepared a statement for this very moment. As the light faded, as microphones were wielded and cameras flashed, catching me in pictures you can still see online today, I began to speak.

'This nightmare has lasted for over thirty years. It should never have been so difficult to bring the truth out. I am so relieved that justice has at last been done. The judge in this case has told me that today is the first day of the rest of my life, and although I don't know how to live my life without the seemingly endless fight against my childhood abusers, I am most certainly looking forward to a future without it . . . and them.'

And that was it. The press packed away their cameras, flipped closed their notebooks, turned and walked away, leaving me alone with my thoughts. I remember thinking, Memo to self: next time you do a *Newsnight* documentary secretly filming and exposing your paedophile stepfather and his friends, try to make it so that the resulting court-case verdict takes place in the middle of the day, because it ain't half lonely out here on these cold concrete steps.

We call it 'disclosing'. It's what you do when you tell. When you go to someone official – a policeman, a teacher, a child-protection professional – and find the strength to tell them what has happened to you.

For most victims of child sexual abuse, especially those abused by a family member or a family friend, finally breaking that wall of secrecy is the most difficult thing they will ever do. For me, at certain times during my childhood, enduring the abuse seemed easier then telling.

Given how hard it is to tell, you'd think that there would be services in place to help care for those that do it, wouldn't you?

You'd be wrong. For a start, if you disclose to the police, you limit your opportunities for counselling, because what you've said to them becomes police evidence. So if and when your case comes to court, everything you say to a counsellor is available to the defence and they'll tear it apart (sorry – 'carefully analyse it') in order to destroy your credibility as a witness (apologies – 'see that justice is done'). For example, let's say you tell the police in your statement, 'I was in a blue room and the offender tore off my skirt', but then don't mention the blue room to your counsellor, the next thing you know you're being accused of giving different versions of the same story.

Rather than see the case fall apart under these circum-stances, the CPS advise against victim counselling. So by disclosing, you're actually cutting off your access to help. Think about it. After all those years of having to hide what's happened to you – the threats, the pressure, the guilt – you finally squeeze that poison out of you . . . and discover you can't tell another living soul.

It was in the wake of the *Newsnight* documentary, when the police finally began taking my allegations seriously, that I realised there is no aftercare for those who find the strength to tell. If you buy a computer, you get some kind of deal to ring the helpline free for six months, just to help you get started. If you disclose details of serious sexual abuse, however, there's no helpline. It's just, 'Thanks for telling us. Now could you keep quiet about it while we put on wigs and argue in court?'

And Victim Support? Don't get me started. OK, too late, I'm started. The thing about Victim Support is that they're fine – great, even – if you've just had your car nicked or your house burgled and you feel fearful or displaced, but they're just not geared up for the kind of crimes we're talking about here. Take my own experience. Victim Support didn't even advise me I could make a financial claim to the CICA (the Criminal Injuries Compensation Authority); instead, an ex-copper sat opposite me for an hour telling me how in tune he was with victims because he used to be a policeman. That was it, end of support. True, my experience was a bad one, and at the very least Victim Support will show victims how to fill in the CICA form, but even that process can't usually begin until after the investigation is concluded or a trial reaches a verdict. There's precious little in the aftercare department. Not a lot to look forward to for those disclosing details of sexual abuse.

It gets worse. In order for the police to make their case as watertight as possible, they form two teams: one whose job it is to prove your case and one whose job it is to disprove your case. If you were to speak to a policeman, I guess they wouldn't describe it in that way, but that's how it feels to a victim. What they do is try the case from the defence's point of view in order to identify any holes.

Think about it objectively and it makes sound legal practice, but from the perspective of the victim, it's devastating to get a call from a policeman who behaves like he doesn't believe you. He's trying to prove the case against you, and he's doing it by cross-examining you, forcing you to question the truth, trying to catch you out, making you feel like a liar. The police check your family, friends, neighbours, old workplaces and addresses, to see if there is anything that can be held against you in a court of law. When it happened to me, I felt so invaded – what in God's name did things I'd done as an adult have to do with being abused as a child?

Apart from the fact that all this stuff is available to the defence – which is a bit like handing bullets to enemy soldiers if you ask me – it makes you, the victim, feel like crap. It happened to me, and though I knew it was necessary and vital and even good practice to build a solid legal case, I still felt attacked and disbelieved. The experience made me distraught, yet I wasn't really able to seek help.

The whole process left me in bits. The judicial system had dragged vile, fossilised memories from me, forced me to confront events locked away deep in my psyche, and afterwards the authorities simply said goodbye and left me to get on with it.

I truly do understand why it has to work like that. It's not the police's fault or even the fault of the Crown Prosecution Service; it's just the way the system works. The trouble is, by the time you are allowed to talk to someone, it's often too late and there are new problems, like self-medication, self-harm and battered self-esteem.

In my case, the self-harm was comfort eating. I almost remember deciding to eat myself ugly, so that I wouldn't attract unwelcome attention. It's one of the stupidest things I have ever done to myself, something that was so easy to do, but now feels almost impossible to undo. I've put my life at risk. Then there's my crushed hip, spastic uterus, flashbacks, obsessive-compulsive disorder, hyper-vigilance/ smell/audio and taste, the hyperhidrosis and the agro-sociophobia, so you can imagine life can be a little tricky at times. So please don't think that I walked away from everything unscathed. I didn't and I would now love to find a way to undo the harm I have done to myself because of them.

This brings me back to the steps of Liverpool Crown Court, because nowhere were the frailties of the system more apparent than in the case of my stepfather and his associates. Standing there that night, I was painfully aware of the shortcomings of our justice system. I didn't realise it then, but standing alone there, once the journalists had left, the kernel of an idea for Phoenix was already beginning to form in my mind. I was thinking, there ought to be more help for us, for people like me, people who manage to tell. Surely this can't be it?

When I'd embarked on this mission, it was to stop Claridge and the others from abusing even more children, once and for all. Me, I'd been abused. I was already broken. But there were other children, a new generation in need of rescue. That's the thing about paedophiles – they don't stop with you. When you're too old for them, they move on to somebody younger. Sometimes they even wait for you to breed them a younger victim; if not stopped, the abuse can carry on down the generations like this.

For that reason, I had known that doing the *Newsnight* documentary would create enormous seismic aftershocks. For example, anybody whose child had ever had contact with Claridge or the others would now be asking them- selves, did they do it to my child? They would see him on the telly or gazing out at them from a newspaper, like some kind of Jabba the Hutt in a cable-knit sweater, and wonder, oh my God, did that monster hurt my child? Consequently, when the programme was aired, the BBC set up helplines. What happened? Meltdown. The system crashed due to the volume of calls.

The ramifications, I realised, were going to be enor- mous. The saddest thing of all, though, was that any help for Stanley's victims had to stop the moment the docu- mentary was broadcast and the police stepped in. So at the very point when victims found the courage to disclose, all possibility of help disappeared. Their real problems were just beginning, and it wasn't one victim – lots and lots of victims were coming forward and disclosing, and there was nothing and nobody out there to help them. I was sad for them, but there seemed no other option.

I had, in my own way, been doing this kind of work

for years and I knew what happened when you told. Before the trial, I'd done what you might describe as secret advocacy – what Sara and I do now, only without the website. I wasn't in the Yellow Pages or anything, but I did it. I'll give you an example: a friend told me about another friend who knew this family. In this family was a twelve-year-old girl – let's call her Jessica. After her cousin had a miscarriage, Jessica wouldn't stop crying, sobbing and beating her chest. Naturally, the family became concerned about the severity of her reaction, and there must have been other concerns, too – the kind of concerns that make you think of someone like me, because I was asked to meet and talk to this girl. From the moment we met, I knew that something major was wrong.

'Look,' I said to her, 'you can go through some really bad things in life. Adults can be really confusing, but I found that when I felt confused by the grown-ups, the best thing to do was to talk about it with someone I trusted.'

It's our mantra. You'll see it on our website. If you close this book knowing just one thing, please let it be this: the only way to stop it is to find a way to tell.

Within an hour of speaking to Jessica, she'd disclosed that her father, her grandfather and all three of her brothers were sexually abusing her and had been for years. She looked forlorn, truly lost. She loved them. That was why she didn't want to tell on them. She didn't want to get them into trouble.

You want to reach out at a time like that, to take that little girl into your arms. You want to protect her, show her what love *really* is – tell her that it's not this horrible corruption of the word forced on her by men whose job it was to protect her but who had abused their power, abused the unconditional love she gave them, taken all that was precious in her life and destroyed it.

'Listen,' I said to her, 'if you love your father, your brothers and your granddad the way you say you do, you need to help them. They can't stop on their own; they need your help to stop, which takes a lot of love. The question is, do you love them enough to do that? Because the only way to do it is to tell the police what you've told me. The police will help you stop them from doing that to you anymore, and there are people out there who will help them learn how to love you properly.'

I reached her. That night, she and her mother went to the police, and that night, the abuse stopped. I stayed in contact with the mother through it all, knowing that the only help I could give was to get the daughter away from her abusers. Back then, though, it was just me, operating via word of mouth and through friends of friends. There was nothing set up, no official service.

Coming back to Stanley, in many ways the court case gave me some closure. Getting the truth out was a big deal for me. With the guilty verdict went the sheer outrage I had felt that the authorities, that society had found it easier to believe the abusers' lies about me than recognise their crimes against me. After everything that had happened, I should have been feeling like it was all over, done and dusted. So how come I didn't? Why did it feel as though justice wasn't enough?

Because it just wasn't enough. There were so many victims who never got justice, never got the help or the support they needed. I felt partly responsible for bringing the media and the police to their door. Afterwards, they couldn't get the help needed, and I promise you all it was not for the want of trying – it simply wasn't available.

Deep down, I think I knew back then that the court case wasn't the end of this fight – it was the beginning of a different fight, a fight for the right to survive and thrive past the abusers, past the justice system and past the lack of help.

These were just some of the thoughts running through my mind as I stood on the steps of Liverpool Crown Court that night. There were so many things I wanted to change, but I had no idea how. So I made my way home to take refuge in the love and care of my own family.

2

After the court case, it took me forty-eight hours to recover enough to face all the correspondence I had received. I'd let it pile up while I'd collected myself, and in my office were postbags full of letters. When I opened my email box, it was full. My answering machine was in meltdown. I had literally thousands of messages, many passed to me by the BBC and the One in Four team.

I started working my way through them. Not that I knew it then, but I was doing my first day of work as a Phoenix advocate. I was receiving questions about the trial and about Stanley. What's happened to him? When's he being sentenced? What about the others? What will they get? They did this to me – what do I do? Who do I tell?

At first I thought, how come the authorities aren't telling them all of this? I realised that they were only telling me because I came to the table with the *Newsnight* team behind me. Plus, I had changed: I wasn't letting the authorities palm me off any longer.

Just looking at the sheer volume of correspondence, I gulped. I felt lost. I couldn't answer every letter or every email. I couldn't phone everybody up – I couldn't afford to. I wasn't an authority on this: all I did was help make the BBC documentary happen to stop Stanley and the

others. I wasn't a policeman, a crown prosecutor, a solicitor, a social worker, a housing or benefits officer, nor
was I a doctor or a counsellor. Some people were asking
questions about things I had no answers to; even those I
thought I could answer were mainly based on my own
personal experiences. These were such important issues
– what if I told someone the wrong thing? What if my
advice just made things worse? I was so afraid of getting
it wrong.

I didn't have the time, the money or the knowledge to
deal with all this stuff one-on-one or face-to-face. It was
then that the idea came to me. Put it this way, if I was a
cartoon Shy, a light bulb would have just gone on over
my head. Despite not knowing how, I decided to set up
a website. I would find the answers to as many of the
questions as I could and publish them online for all to
see, and that's what I did. I got my head round buying a
domain and building a two-page website, and I set it up.

At first, it mainly involved helping those from Operation
Phoenix, so I called it PhoenixSurvivors.com – it was all
about sharing information after the case: the sentencing,
what victims could do next and so on. The next step was
learning to help the victims in other areas of their lives.
Trouble paying bills? I'd be on the phone to the electricity
company: 'With the victim's consent, let me give you some
background to the problems this person is having, to see
if you can help them.' Housing issues? I'd be on the case:
'This particular family were witnesses in a large court
case. As a result of that, they've become isolated from
their neighbours. Despite the fact that they're the victims,
not the offenders, there's been some bad feeling. I think

it's important that you move them because we're in the middle of a follow-up to the BBC's groundbreaking *Newsnight* documentary and obviously we want to say that you did absolutely everything you could to help them.'

Whereas before I'd been advocating secretly, now I'd introduce myself as the Phoenix Chief Advocate Shy Keenan. Before long other people started coming on board to assist me and I had volunteers helping me turn the website into something more user-friendly. Now my two-page website became a ten-page website. It was starting to look dead professional, and all the time I was receiving more and more emails asking for help. Now, though, I knew a little about how to help them, because I was learning as I went along. I'd receive emails like 'My foster parents sexually abused me when I was ten. I ran away and never went back, and I've never lived anywhere near them since. They lived in Scotland. Is it still possible to tell the police what happened?'

'Yes, it is,' I could tell them. 'All you need to do is put together as much information as you can remember, including any names and addresses. Then you need to go and speak to the police in the area where it happened.'

Another email would ask, 'Is it illegal to have sex with my brother if we are both consenting adults?'

'Yes, it bloody well is.'

Or, 'I was abused by our old neighbour. We've moved twice since, and they've moved as well. If I don't know where they are now, can I still tell the police?'

'Yes, you can still tell the police. Don't worry – they will trace them.'

Or, 'I was sexually abused when I was abroad living

with an adopted family. I recently told the police, but they don't believe me and won't listen. What do I do?'

'Leave it with me.'

I would make calls and talk to the police. Through that I gained contacts in the force. As a result, I started receiving calls from them. 'We've got an eleven-year-old victim here. We've asked her about sex with her stepfather and she's just clammed up – won't talk to us. Have you got any guidance for us?'

I told them the problem was the way the question was being asked: 'Have *you* been having sex with your stepfather?' The question should be 'Has your stepfather been having any kind of sexual relations with you?' It's all about a change of emphasis, so the victim doesn't immediately feel that he or she might be to blame in some way. They took it on board, the child opened up, the police came back, said thank you and all of a sudden my contacts in the police had become friends in the police, and they had someone they could turn to when they needed help.

Tracing people from the past was a theme of many of the emails I received, so I decided to take a course as a private investigator to enable me to do it better. The tutors were just brilliant. They helped me every step of the way and I felt so proud when I passed – my first academic achievement.

Another time, someone from the Home Office called me. 'We have a problem with the media's perception of such-and-such. Is there any advice you can give us?' Then they asked, 'Can you come in and give a talk to offer our people some insight on how we need to work with victims?'

Gradually, my profile was growing, but it was to be a

lonely time – one of the loneliest of my life. It's not work anyone should do alone – unsupported, it can literally smash your soul to pieces – but there was nobody else for these people to turn to. What's more, it cost money. My phone bills were huge. Plus, I had to pay for equipment, the Internet, the domain name. And of course, when you're a victim of child sex abuse, you tend to have a strange relationship with money – certainly if, like me, you'd been pimped out by your abusers. Asking for money feels wrong, so I didn't seek funding. Besides, society doesn't really like it when the words 'victim' and 'money' feature in the same sentence. There's an element of shame. I didn't know it at the time, but finding the funds to carry on the work would be an ongoing daily struggle.

All the time, I was learning my craft with Phoenix. I was learning about the system, its weaknesses and strengths. I was learning about bureaucracy and law. Little did I know it then, but at the same time – and not too far away as the crow flies – Sara was learning hers.

3

One day, Sara was in the supermarket with her little girl, Ellie, who was born after Sarah died. They were wandering along the fruit and veg aisle, Sara pushing the trolley, Ellie trotting beside her, burbling, muttering about nothing in particular and doing it the way kids do that makes you wish you could record it to listen to for all time.

For such a tiny one – she's four – Ellie's as sharp as a tack, full of questions. It wasn't long before she started to recognise the little girl she saw in newspapers or flash up on TV as being Sarah, the same little girl she saw in photographs at home.

She began asking her mum questions about Sarah. Because of the public profile of the case, Sara never had to make a choice about whether or not to shield the children from the truth. Sara promised them that if they asked a question, she would answer truthfully and Ellie was no exception. She already knew that she had two big sisters, one who was alive and one who was in Heaven. She knew that a bad man had taken Sarah away. What she didn't understand was why.

'Mummy,' she asked in the supermarket that day, 'why did the bad man take Sarah away?'

It came out of the blue and it took Sara's breath away. She didn't have an answer at first, other than to give her little girl a hug. Then, after a few moments, she mustered a reassuring face and told Ellie that there were some bad people in this world who did bad things. She told her that this particular bad person was now in jail for ever and couldn't hurt anyone anymore and that Ellie was safe.

Inside, Sara was sobbing. It's the question that beats her up: *why?* Why did Whiting drive down that road, at that time, on that day? Why didn't she do this, rather than that? Why did their paths have to cross? Why?

Across the country on that very day, there were a million parents who had said yes to their children. Yes, you can pop down the road to the shop to buy some sweets. Yes, you can go play with your friends in the park across the way. Yes, you can walk to Nanny's with your sister or brother. And everything was as it should have been. Everything was fine.

But not for Sara and her family. Not at that moment, in that place, at that time. Whiting had turned this normal, everyday decision into every parent's nightmare come horrifyingly true.

It took the help and support of an outstanding team of trauma counsellors and support workers to help the family cope with what Whiting had done to them. That team were with the Paynes all the way from when Sarah went missing until after her heartbreaking funeral.

And yet here's the strange, amazing thing about Sara. Sarah was kidnapped and killed by a paedophile. Next, Sara lost her brother to lung cancer and then her mother (Sara believes that the shock of what happened to Sarah literally killed her mother). Then Sara lost her father to a genetic aneurysm. It has been a terrible decade for Sara, yet when asked about what happened after Sarah died, do you know what she says?

'I'm lucky.'

'Come again?'

'I am, Shy,' she tells me. 'When it comes to being the parent of a murdered child, I am, in some ways, one of the lucky ones. I was lucky Whiting was found and arrested. I was lucky that they found the DNA and that he was given life. I was lucky that I had Sussex Police dealing with it, because they're a bloody good police force and the best family-liaison officers. I was lucky because the press wanted to help us. It was luck because I have since met plenty more who did not get anything like the same help and support that we were given. Plenty.'

'Does it ever get any easier?' The question came from a woman Sara met at one of the Britain's Children's Champion Award dinners. The woman's daughter had been shot. All she wanted from Sara was some reassurance that at some point the hurt was going to ease, that one day she'd wake up and the anguish would somehow have receded.

'I'm sorry, I wish I could tell you different, but it never does,' Sara replied. 'Some days it's worse than others, but it never gets easier. All I can say is that maybe the body adapts. Like you lose a leg and after a while your body just gets used to operating with only one leg. Perhaps it's the same with grief. But no, you never stop grieving. You never stop mourning.'

One Christmas Eve, Sara saw someone she recognised. It was completely unexpected; all of a sudden this young lad approached and he looked familiar, except not, and for a second or so Sara struggled to place him. Then she did. He was one of Sarah's school friends, only he was older than she remembered. Eight years older. Not frozen in time the way Sarah is, a pretty little eight-year-old girl smiling in a school photograph. This was a sixteen-year-old boy, the same age Sarah would have been but for Whiting.

'Are you all right about it, hon?' I asked her later.

'Yeah. You know, I just came home and had a little cry, just went off for a bit and shed a few tears.'

There are certain triggers. She always has a rough July and August. She just about functions, but those two months dredge up the events of July and August 2000 and it's almost too much to bear. She used to drink to dull the pain, but not anymore: she's got her other children and little Ellie to think about. Another tough time is Sarah's birthday, of course, 13 October, but also Christmas, probably Sarah's favourite time of year. For a girl who loved life as much as Sarah did, you can imagine how important Christmas was.

'She loved celebrations, Shy, that was the thing,' Sara told me once. 'Birthdays, Christmas, Halloween. She was always the one organising things, making costumes, putting up decorations. So to celebrate Christmas without her is hard. It's really hard. We all know that what she'd want more than anything is for us to carry on and have a great Christmas, but sometimes that makes it harder, because she's not here to give us a kick up the arse.'

Sara goes to the grave about twice a year, but never on anniversaries. Sometimes the press will be there to try and catch a picture of her at the graveside and she doesn't want that. Family members tend it regularly, keep it neat and tidy. She says that whenever she goes, it always looks nice.

We compare battle scars. Like me, Sara suffers from post-traumatic stress. She gets flashbacks, nightmares, and her short-term memory is shot, unlike mine. Sometimes when we talk over Skype, she will be hunched over, tired and haggard. I want to scream, 'Get to bed, girl! Can't you see you need to rest?' I want to reach through the computer screen and somehow cross the miles and give her a cuddle.

She'd most likely tell me to bugger off if I did, though – neither of us is the touchy-feely type when we're upset. This isn't some fragile little flower we're talking about here. My best friend is armour-plated. Simply the calmest, most determined person I've ever met, and believe me, I've met a few.

Sometimes I wonder about the work we both do. It means we can never, ever hide from our past. Every day we have our metaphorical scabs ripped off to reveal fresh, glistening wounds beneath. We allow it, in the hope that those who don't know will learn and help us change things for the better.

'It's like I've got a partition in my head,' she told me one day. 'I've got Sarah here on one side, and she's the real Sarah. She's my daughter Sarah. And somehow I manage to keep her separate from this other Sarah, who's the girl in the papers, the girl behind Sarah's Law. She's the one who's doing all of this.'

'How do you mean?'
'I mean when Whiting picked on Sarah, he picked on the wrong girl – the wrong family.'

4

It was on 17 July 2000 that everything changed for Sara. That was the day she was told that Sarah had been found. Before that, she and her family were just too dazed and frightened to think beyond Sarah's safe return. Then came the news they all dreaded, and at that moment Sara went from frightened to determined – determined that this would not happen to another family. Not if she could help it.

She began learning about paedophiles; she learned things that weren't public knowledge at that time. If Sarah's death marked the moment a nation lost its innocence, then that's because there were a great many truths about sex offenders that had remained hidden, undisturbed like silt in a stagnant lake, and it took Sarah's murder, then Sara's persistence, to stir up some of that filth. She brought paedophiles on to the news agenda.

Think about it. Pre-Sara, there had been various scandals in the 1970s, mainly involving child abuse at children's homes. Before and after, though, sex offenders stayed under the radar: nobody talked about them; nobody even dared to say the word 'paedophile' in case they got accused of being one. When a child was abducted and murdered, no one ever asked why.

Sarah's death and Sara's subsequent campaign changed

all of that. As a parent, she was unafraid to confront Whiting's motives for kidnapping and killing Sarah. She brought it to the public's attention that he was a paedophile. Meanwhile, she discovered that there were an awful lot of people like Whiting about – there were 350,000 convicted sex offenders living in the UK in 2000, of whom about 110,00 had abused children. She learned that 64 per cent of convicted sex offenders will reoffend (numbers have since increased), that the average paedophile could potentially abuse up to a hundred children throughout their career, and that six or seven kids were murdered every year in sexually motivated attacks in the UK.

She also remembered a news story she'd read years ago, and she looked into it again. It was a story about Megan Kanka, a seven-year-old girl who lived in New Jersey. In 1994, she was kidnapped, raped and murdered by a violent sex offender, Jesse Timmendequas, who had moved into a house opposite the family. After Megan's death, her parents argued that had they known about this guy's history, they would have taken steps to keep Megan away from him.

Why, they wanted to know, were they not warned of the danger living opposite? After all, you get a warning on an apple pie. 'Caution: contents may be hot.' You're told that a packet of nuts 'may contain nuts'. That herbal sleeping pills 'may cause drowsiness'. Why not that a child rapist has just moved in opposite your family? 'Caution: may kidnap, rape and kill your child.'

The Kankas began a petition demanding the right to know if a sexual predator had moved into the area. It was the parents' right, they argued. Why should something like that be kept a secret? Almost half a million signatures later, Megan's Law was passed in the state of New Jersey. The following year, a nationwide law was passed that required every state to follow New Jersey's lead.

As a result, the American Department of Justice launched the National Sex Offender Public Website. Go there and you can search by name, state, county or zip code and call up details of offenders, complete with pictures. Believe me, you have never seen a more motley group of mugshots in your life than on this site. Have a look for yourself online – Google it. All of a sudden, these guys don't appear so scary. Stick them on this website and the mystique fades. They look like any other creepy cowards.

Megan's Law struck at the very heart of every paedophile's most effective weapon: the culture of keeping secrets. They call it their 'human rights'; we call it their 'inhuman rights'.

The UK response to the Megan Kanka case was to set up the Sex Offenders Register. It meant that sex offenders were required to sign the register on leaving prison, so in theory the police, probation and social services could monitor their movements. However, there was no public access to the register, nor were any of the agencies allowed to pass on information about it. So if a concerned policeman saw a local single mum taking up with a known sex offender, he would be breaching the sex offender's rights to inform her. But the fact that a paedophile was watching *Match of the Day* on her sofa? It was not the single mother's right to know. On top of that, the register wasn't retrospective, so only included those convicted after 1997.

Sara's eyes were opened by all this research, so when the *News of the World* called wanting an interview and offering cash, she made them an offer. The family had decided not to do any exclusives or take money for interviews, she told them, but would the *News of the World* look into Megan's Law?

'If you've got any ideas about how we can do something like that in the UK, then get back to me,' she told the reporter, Robert Kellaway.

A day or so later and the paper had come up with a proposal: a campaign called 'For Sarah', the aim of which would be to press for the introduction of Sarah's Law, which included a whole package of measures aimed at protecting children. Central to it was giving parents the right to know if convicted sex offenders were living near their children.

The paper kicked off the campaign by 'naming and shaming' convicted paedophiles, which was when the you-know-what hit the fan. Naming and shaming split the country right down the middle. The man in the street seemed to be behind the campaign, whereas the broadsheet newspapers were less keen – even in the face of a MORI poll showing 98 per cent of people believed that parents had a right to know if there was a paedophile living near them.

Not so helpful to the 'For Sarah' campaign was a wave of headline-grabbing vigilante-style incidents. There were cases of mistaken identity and a very lively demonstration on the Paulsgrove estate in Portsmouth, with the crowd targeting the home of a paedophile called Victor Burnett. Sara later learned that the incident had nothing to do with their campaign – the demonstration had been planned for some time – but feelings were clearly running high in the wake of Sarah's murder. Then there was a much-quoted incident in which the home of a paediatrician was daubed with graffiti – again used as a stick with which to beat the campaign. There were two alleged suicides, death threats were issued to *News of the World* staff, the editor, Rebekah Wade, had to have a bodyguard, and the News International building was evacuated during a bomb scare.

It was a brilliant start to the campaign.

No, honest, it really was. It might not have been subtle and it may have had some distressing consequences, but it didn't half get the job done. Suddenly, child sexual abuse, paedophiles and their movements and the public right to know became hot topics.

Why? Because the issues could no longer be ignored.

'I was one of the first parents to openly acknowledge that their child had been abducted and killed for sexual reasons,' Sara said late one night, staring out of the computer screen at me.

Even to hear her say it was shocking, mainly because I knew it was true. When Sarah's body was found, she was in a terrible state. Sara learned some things about the condition of her daughter that no parent should ever hear about their child. Sarah had lain outside for some time and animals had got at the body. The post-mortem showed that she had been strangled or suffocated, but there was not enough of her to prove she had been raped. Nevertheless, Sara never tried to pretend her daughter had been abducted for anything other than sexual reasons.

This is not to say that other victims' parents do, but simply that Sara refused to let the issue be sidelined. Because she was brave enough to confront that fact, she got the general public to confront it, too.

True, there may have been some hysteria surrounding the naming-and-shaming campaign of 2000, and you can debate its merits until the cows come home, but let's be clear about this, the *News of the World* team really cared. They believed in the campaign and they backed Sara to the hilt, which makes them and their readers heroes in our book. They stuck to their guns, and thanks to them, the campaign made its point loud and clear. And not just for the man on the street, either. After a fortnight of naming and shaming, and with Sarah's murder still fresh in people's minds, a meeting was called.

Attending were the *News of the World*, Mike and Sara, the Association of Chief Police Officers, the NSPCC and the Association of Chief Officers of Probation. It was one of the first times – if not the very first time – that representatives of those groups had all sat round a table to discuss child protection. After four hours, it ended with all sides agreeing to draw up a charter for Sarah's Law. The meeting had been sparked by the *News of the World*'s naming-and-shaming campaign and fuelled by Sara's bravery, by her need to do something in the wake of her daughter's death, and it was to have the most far-reaching consequences for child protection this country has ever seen. You go, girl.

5

Afterwards, with Sara and the *News of the World* agreeing to suspend the naming-and-shaming campaign, the paper's lawyers went away and drew up the Sarah's Law charter. This was the document that would show the way forward.

It had three main aims. The first was to give parents the power to protect their kids from paedophiles by giving them 'controlled access' to information about individuals in their neighbourhood, including convicted child sex offenders who 'may pose a risk to their child'. That was the headline-grabbing bit, the bit people understand as being Sarah's Law.

The second aim of the charter was to help victims of sexual abuse, giving courts the power to 'prevent offenders contacting or living near their victims'. It went on to say the release conditions should include restrictions on contact with victims, and that every 'victim of child sexual abuse should receive appropriate support, counselling and therapy', plus that victims should be kept 'in the loop' when it came to the sentence. In other words, they should understand the process and be kept informed of what period 'in custody' the offender would serve and when they would be released.

The third aim was to try and improve our approach to the prevention of abuse. So for a start 'the existing vetting arrangements for people intending to work with children should be extended to cover all voluntary organisations' and to try and make it easier for these guys to get the info without massive costs. This was the hope at least.

Added to that, the charter asked for changes to be made to the Sex Offenders Register. These changes have since been actioned. In 1997, for example, signing on to the register was a fairly ad hoc affair and could even be done by proxy. One of the changes Sara was able to make in the early years of the 'For Sarah' campaign was that offenders had to visit a police station in person within forty-eight hours of their release from prison, or within forty-eight hours of changing address.

Furthermore, the charter stipulated that photographs should be taken as part of the registration process and again if the offender's appearance changed – not just once. Now offenders must have a new picture taken whenever they sign, annually or when they change address. They should also be subject to regular risk assessments. Those with severe personality disorders should be kept in secure accommodation. The other stipulation of being on the register is that you can't leave the country without first notifying the authorities.

In short, the charter was a huge, far-reaching outline for the future of child protection. All from that one meeting.

'We sat in that room,' Sara told me, 'and worked on what we all needed to do in order to do the job better. The people in the room all agreed to Sarah's Law and agreed to back it. After the *News of the World* and their legal teams had written up the charter, it was about this thick.' She held up her hands, showing something that was very thick. 'We got a barrister and legal experts to go through it. Then we got all the people in the room to sign it and gave it to the home secretary at the time, Jack Straw.'

Next, the Home Office went through the charter, saying which bits they would accept and which they wouldn't: 'This we think we can get through, but we'll never get the Lords to agree to that bit.' It went backwards and forwards. Some points were the subject of various meetings all over the country.

After all the petitioning and campaigning, Jack Straw drew up the Criminal Justice and Court Services Act 2000, which contained many amendments to the Sex Offenders Act 1997.

It was a great start. New laws were brought in to stop paedophiles working with kids, sex-abuse victims were to be kept informed when their abuser left jail. (It didn't happen before then. Can you believe it?) There was an increase in maximum penalties for the possession of indecent images of children, and new laws were introduced that allowed the police to proactively protect children – not just reactively. Other immediate changes to the law involved the police's powers of re-arrest, new restrictions on sex offenders' movements – stopping them hanging around schools, pools and parks – and further aspects of the process that involved managing and monitoring offenders. The sort of stuff Sara had assumed happened automatically but didn't.

All positive.

Even better, shortly after that came MAPPA. Or, to give

it its full title, Multi-Agency Public Protection Arrangements, an offender-management team that was, at the time, the government answer to Sarah's Law. The idea was that the local police, probation and prison services would join forces to form a panel, working with health, housing, education and social services. It's the panel's job to draw up a risk-assessment and management plan for offenders living within the community. The various agencies would share information, so if the police have specific intelligence about an offender, they will pass it on to, say, social services. The idea is that each offender has an individual management programme. So, for example, if an offender has previous form for hanging around toilets and is barred by the courts from doing so, then each agency on the MAPPA team will be aware of this. What if our offender turns his attention to swimming pools? Then the case goes back before the MAPPA team, who will apply to the court to get an order banning him from swimming pools.

Before MAPPA, you'd have a lone probation officer who might have to deal with a hundred sex offenders and five different agencies. The offenders would come in every so often – depending on their parole restrictions – to talk. The probation officer would only be able to use their professional intuition to assess any risk. In other words, the probation officer might ask, 'Have you done any offending lately? Been chasing any kids? Anything like that?' 'No,' the offender would say. 'I'm over all that malarkey. Don't know what came over me.' If there was no evidence to the contrary, the probation officer would be forced to assess them as 'low risk' and ask to see them again in a few months' time. Even if the probation officer did have any concerns, they would face an uphill battle to get all the agencies 'in a row' to take the right action. Now, however, the probation officer would have a proactive MAPPA team to turn to, to back them up.

Before MAPPA, once an offender's probation period ended, they were essentially left to their own devices. If a child went missing locally, they might have received a knock on the door, but otherwise nothing. Now, though, you're assessed by a MAPPA panel and you stay on the register once you've finished your probation. Sorry, but you do. Plus, high-risk offenders can expect a knock on the door and a visit at least once a month.

In short, sex offenders are now monitored. And that's largely down to Sara and the meeting brought about by the *News of the World*.

Of course, MAPPA had its teething problems to begin with, as Sara soon found out. It's one thing to get high-ranking representatives from the agencies involved in a high-profile meeting organised by the country's bestselling Sunday newspaper. It's quite another to get the rank and file talking. At first, they couldn't get the agencies to work together, so for example social services wouldn't work with probation, who wouldn't work with the prisons, and none of them would work with the police. All of these guys work for the greater good, but they all came to the table with their own agenda specific to their own organisation. Sara worked on it, though – they all did – and gradually things began to improve. Years later and we've come a long way.

'We're looking at a different world now, Shy, right across

the board,' said Sara recently. 'You wouldn't believe it, but it's like officialdom is finally working together. We're finally moving away from "wait and see".'

One of the things that first struck Sara was this wait-and-see policy. Not that it was officially called that, you understand, but that was what Sara came to call it, because instead of being proactive when it came to stopping sex offenders (who have a very high reoffending rate, remember), we were sticking them back into society and keeping quiet until they did it again.

Sara explained, 'You could have a sex offender with a very long record who kept on repeating that offence, kept on going back to prison, kept getting let out. The police would see them around – possibly about to reoffend – and not be able to do anything about it. The offender might be near a child and the police wouldn't be able to tell the child's family because of the offender's right to privacy.'

That has now changed. 'Today, if you have an offender who has picked up children from a playground before and the authorities see them hanging around a playground, they can move them on. They can tell them not to be there. If they see them going into houses where there are children, they can stop them. Before, they had no power to do that. There was no power of arrest unless they had committed an offence. There was no power to stop them from going wherever they wanted. Because of the offender's right to privacy, the police's hands were very much tied.'

While the central request of Sarah's Law – that parents have the right to access information about sex offenders

living in their area – had not been addressed, one conces-
sion had been made. The police were given the power to
hand information on offenders to organisations working
with children. It wasn't all that Sara wanted – not by any
means – but it was a step in the right direction.

'They finally had the power to use common sense when
it came to sex offenders,' she told me one night.

It's our belief that you can't 'cure' paedophilia; it's a
sexual preference. They do what they do because they
want to and because they *can*. There is nothing anyone
can do about the 'want to' part of this statement, but
there is a lot we can do about the 'can'. We can all do
whatever we legally can do to get in their way. The biggest
deterrent for paedophiles has never really been the law;
the biggest deterrent is those who use the rule of law to
stop them. You can't fight what you can't see, so the more
people who know, the better we will be at stopping
paedophiles. Empowering people with both the knowledge and the law was really what was needed. The changes
to the law took all of this into account and were a major
improvement.

People think of Sarah's Law as 'that thing where you
can find out where paedos live', and yes, that's part it.
But it was and is so much more. The work Sara's done
under Sarah's Law has changed the whole landscape of
child protection in the UK. And it all began with Sarah.

6

So, you see, we were a natural fit, Sara and me. Both of us had had our eyes tragically opened to the way the system treats sex offenders and their victims. It was only right that having come together as friends, we'd join forces in work. And we did. Phoenix was once one, but now it was two.

At first, we were just mates talking through the day's events, which for me was an absolute godsend: long ago, I pledged to keep my work and family separate, so to have someone to talk to about what I was doing was wonderful. We have a certain determination in common, a natural tick-tock to our friendship that works well for us.

We both have major campaigns that we work on, that have each other's full support. The campaign for Sarah's Law is Sara's; mine is to bring in an antidiscrimination law for victims. In addition, at any one time there are always six or seven laws we're both trying to get changed and things we're both trying to promote. Plus the constant struggle for funding to keep Phoenix going. It was a lot to deal with. Sometimes it was too much.

At least there were now two of us. On the phone I'd always introduced myself as the Phoenix Chief Advocate, and now we were the Phoenix Chief Advocates. That little 's' made such a difference to us both.

Working with us are our other Phoenixes and our supporters: an informal voluntary group of people, some of whom have been there themselves, and others who have not but who support what we do. They are an incredible team who come from every walk of life and every kind of profession – indeed, many of them are at the very top of their field. They have always been there for us and we would be nothing without them.

And that was us, the Phoenix Survivors team. Together, we were stronger than ever before, and we began to learn much more about each other. Even though I have a condition that makes it hard for me to get out, we live in an era of high-tech communications gadgetry, so it wasn't too much of a problem and we did our best to work round it. We also did our best to keep each other's spirits up, which is an essential part of the job. We're the people you turn to once some part of the system has failed you. As a result, we don't tend to get a lot of good-news stories on our desks. It can be very defeating and not a little soul-crushing at times, especially those times when a case goes right to the heart.

It wasn't long after Sara and I had teamed up that we had one such case. I'll never forget it. It involved a young girl called Lauren. She was abused by her father and – still a child herself – had his baby. The baby, a girl, died not long after it was born. Because of her age, Lauren was kept out of the burial process; she wasn't even allowed to name the baby. All 'it' was portrayed to her as was a vile but key piece of evidence in the criminal case against her father, who was later jailed. The problem was that nobody had stopped to ask Lauren how she felt about her baby.

More pain was to come. Lauren's mother – a piece of utter pond life – divorced the father, then married another man. Following the trial, Lauren was awarded compensation, which was kept in trust for her by her mother. Together, she and her new husband spent all Lauren's compensation. By the time Lauren was old enough to ask for it, there was none left.

The mother and stepfather were later jailed for stealing Lauren's money, but there was worse to come. Lauren wanted to give her baby a name and wanted the name inscribed on a gravestone. When she tried to do so, however, she found she couldn't because she didn't own the grave – her mother did. When Lauren asked her mother if she could have the grave, she said no. She asked if she could put a stone there, with an inscription, and was again told no. According to her mother, she could not even put flowers on the grave.

See what we mean about pond life?

We helped Lauren get that grave. We can't say exactly how, and it wasn't without a great deal of difficulty, but we did it because we could see that Lauren needed to acknowledge the birth of her child beyond a police evidence bag identifying a crime. She needed to name her child, to grieve for her and to lay her poor little soul to rest, as only a mother can.

Shortly after, we were contacted by Sandra, a mother whose daughter had been abused by a member of the local clergy. When Sandra tried to get the church to do something about it, she soon discovered that religious interests were being placed above those of the children. In short, she was being betrayed by her church.

We got in touch with the church. They should take a closer look at these allegations, we suggested.

It was a one-off mistake and would be dealt with in-house, they rejoined.

Not good enough, we replied. The police should be called in to help clarify the truth of the matter. We also suggested that if not the police, then maybe the media could help them.

Oh, they said, in that case . . .

They decided to work within the law and this one-off abuse case turned into at least nine. With the truth out, the victims and the community have a much better chance of healing, forgiving and helping each other to recover.

Thinking like an advocate involves investigation, troubleshooting, problem-solving and communicating. A lot of what we do is about establishing the facts and the problem; next, it's figuring out what the answer is; then it's tracking down the people responsible for that department and talking to them. Our role is to advocate for the victim, to try and reach a more satisfactory conclusion for them, and this can take weeks, months or even years. Once we commit to a case, we are in it for the long haul.

As Phoenix Survivors, we had an open-door policy when it came to helping victims. Our main task was just victim advocacy. At the same time, all sorts of information landed on our desks, some of which would raise wider concerns. An example of this was when we discovered that sex offenders were being allowed to work as school teachers, so we began campaigning for change. Or when we found out that important child-protection information was being lost, and that offender-management information was not even being filed properly by the government. Or when we uncovered the fact that police services in the UK were being forced to purge their systems of intelligence files over seven years old.

Put it this way, we were never afraid of getting stuck in, and still aren't. What we didn't realise back then, of course, was that our biggest battle wouldn't be against the paedophiles. Our biggest battle would be fighting for the survival of Phoenix Survivors and for all those who reached out to us for help.

7

'I never rehearse, Shy. I never rehearse my speeches.'

Now that we were working together, Sara and I still had some surprises in store for each other, even having been friends for so long – and here was just such a surprise. It turns out that even though Sara regularly gives speeches across the nation, addressing everyone from the public to politicians, from law-makers to the law-enforcers, there's one thing she never does.

'You what?' I gulped back.

'I never rehearse my speeches. I don't even write anything down.'

Just hearing that was enough to give me the fear – me, who writes everything down, who plans meticulously. Sara – the same Sara, remember, who has a terrible short-term memory, a legacy of the stress from all her bereavements – never writes her speeches, or even plans what to say beforehand.

Still, it rarely fails. She once gave a speech to the Police Federation, and that speech, like so much of what she does, changed the law.

At that time, we were campaigning for changes in the child-abduction laws that were essentially based almost exclusively on parental abduction. Our campaign was prompted by a case in which a young girl was the victim of an attempted abduction by a stranger. She was standing close to a park, beside a row of shops, and a known sex offender dragged her into the trees. She screamed blue murder. Some shopkeepers heard the commotion and came running out. The would-be abductor threw his mobile phone at one shopkeeper and took to his toes. The police used the phone to identify the offender and he was prosecuted.

Thankfully, the victim escaped unmolested. Unfortunately, though, because our phone-chucking sex offender had not managed to commit a sex crime, the judge couldn't place him back on the Sex Offenders Register, even though he knew the guy had once been on it and was obviously not attempting to kidnap this young girl in order to hold a conversation with her.

There was another case involving a young girl who was waiting at a bus-stop. A suspected offender tried and failed to abduct her. The incident was caught on CCTV. The guy involved was charged with the crime, but when it came to sentencing, the judge could not put the offender on the Sex Offenders Register because he hadn't managed to commit a sexual offence and the girl had escaped unharmed (all things being relative, obviously: it's pretty disturbing when you know you've come *this close* to being sexually assaulted, perhaps even raped, maybe even killed). This was as frustrating for the judges as it was for us – their hands were tied.

This is a classic example of something we do. We try to identify a problem – something in legislation or in the law – and work out how to get it changed. In this case, we launched a campaign for change in the non-parental child-abduction laws. What we wanted was the law to force the convicted abductor to prove that they had *not* abducted the child for sexual purposes. If they failed to prove this, the court should be allowed (if it sees fit) to place them on the Sex Offenders Register.

To get any changes brought in, you need to be speaking to the right people, so when Sara was asked to give a speech to the Police Federation, she leaped at the chance. As usual, she didn't write anything down or rehearse what she would say; she just took to the stage and spoke to them from her heart.

'It was the rank and file,' she told me later. 'I stood up and I explained to them that Roy Whiting is not a paedophile. They all looked at me aghast. You could see them wondering why I'd said it. So I explained, "Because when he comes out, which one day he will, whether I like it or not, he won't go on to the Sex Offenders Register.'

Everyone in the room shifted uncomfortably. Why wouldn't Roy Whiting, one of the most famous paedophiles in the country, the man who had kidnapped and murdered Sarah Payne, go on the Sex Offenders Register?

'Why?' continued Sara. 'Because we can't *prove* what he did to Sarah. Because of the way she was left, there was insufficient evidence to prove what he did to her. There is no forensic evidence.'

There, in Sara's words, was a concrete example of why the law needed changing. A convicted paedophile was now serving time for child abduction and murder, yet would not be officially recognised as the very dangerous predatory paedophile he is upon his release. It is crucial

that the authorities and the public know the full extent
of the danger that the likes of Whiting actually pose. If
Whiting is not placed on the Sex Offenders Register, then
the right people won't even know about him, let alone be
legally empowered to monitor or stop him. Thanks to
Sara's very high-profile Police Federation speech, the law
has started to change and we sincerely hope that the
changes will be made in time so that the authorities and
the law-empowered public will be able to do much more
to guard themselves against the Roy Whitings of this world.
Given that Whiting received a life sentence with a fifty-
year tariff, we can only hope the world will never have to
worry about this particular monster again.

'See how lucky I am, Shy – I don't have to worry about
him coming out for fifty bloody years.' As I said earlier,
Sara often says that, when it comes to being the parent
of a murdered child, she is one of the lucky ones. She
was lucky that the home secretary gave Whiting such a
long tariff. We both know it doesn't always work that
way, though. Plus, things can always change, and because
of this potential, there is always this nagging 'what if?'.

Sara explained, 'There are loads of legal loopholes that
can get you out of jail early, Shy – things like ill health
and old age. Even overcrowding can trigger early-release
parole hearings these days. You can just imagine him
saying, "I haven't molested a child or murdered anyone
in all the years that I've been in this cell on my own, Your
Honour. See, that's proof I've changed. Haven't I been
punished enough yet, Your Honour?"'

You might wonder how she can joke about something
like that – an imaginary conversation between a judgment

panel and the man who killed her daughter. Well, sometimes it's better to laugh than to cry.

The Sex Offenders Register has come a long way, but
there are other changes we'd like to see. We would like
to see more conditions being placed on those on the register
– much is up to the discretion of the judges, such as being
unable to work with children, or visit swimming pools,
or use computers. What we want is for the register to
come pre-set with those conditions, so that if you're on
the register, you're automatically banned from using the
Internet, and if you have to use the Internet because of
your job, then you'll be monitored.

How, though, do you monitor these guys? When Gary
Glitter (AKA Paul Gadd) returned to the UK last year, all
the talk was of what to do with him, and all the usual argu-
ments reared their ugly heads. On the one side, you get the
death-penalty crowd, who sometimes look to the likes of
us to give them support. Whenever we meet them, we can
see their disappointment upon discovering that we don't
support the public castration or execution of all paedophiles.

'So you don't support the death penalty, then?' I asked
Sara one night, shortly after we became friends.

She shook her head at once. 'No.'

'Not even for Roy Whiting?'

Again she shook her head. She didn't even need to
think about it. 'Not even for Roy Whiting,' she said,
lighting a cigarette.

'OK, then, a hypothetical question: say if the death
penalty was reintroduced tomorrow and it was enforced
for past crimes, so Roy Whiting was to be given the death
penalty, would you campaign against it?'

She exhaled smoke and rested her chin on her arm, thinking for a second. 'I don't know if I'd campaign *against* it – that would be a whole different story – but I don't see how me becoming a murderer would help stop murderers. I get people who come up to me at conferences and they want to know what I think about the death penalty and I tell them the same thing every time: not in my daughter's name you don't.'

What we found when we first became friends was that our conversations never went the same way as any of the debates we were hearing or seeing on the radio or telly. When we watched others discuss offender punishment, management or treatment, it seemed all they would do was talk up an angry storm about various extremes, whether that was capital punishment or tea-and-sympathy treatment programmes. Where, we wondered, was the middle ground?

Because what we knew was that sex offenders exploit the crap out of the tea-and-sympathy lot, and the string-'em-up-and-shoot-them-dead brigade no doubt make great copy and great radio and television fodder, but they're not what we're about, and frankly, they don't help bring this fight against paedophiles any further forward – if anything, their anger helps sex offenders. We call these people 'the tail-chasers'. All they can think about is that they want paedophiles hung, drawn, quartered, tarred and feathered, and the fact that the country won't do that angers them. Anger clouds judgement; paedophiles encourage and exploit clouded judgements. They shout louder and louder and get redder and redder in the face and never let us get a word in edgeways. Maybe if they would just stay calm for a moment, we could tell them about some of the solutions we do have, like ROM: Remote Offender Monitoring.

This was something we came up with on a train, believe it or not. Sara was on the train, on her way into London for a meeting, and I was at home. As usual, we were chatting away, trying to find ways of actually putting the world to rights, instead of grumbling about how bad things are. We were talking about GPS systems for cars. I'd seen something on TV about how police helicopters use GPS tracker devices to tell them that a car has been stolen and where it is. I went on to tell Sara about a paedophile I once spoke to.

'He was telling me that the only way to stop him reoffending was to sellotape a probation officer to his arse.'

'Not a bad idea,' said Sara. 'But what we need is some kind of sellotape substitute.'

'Yeah, like GPPS – Global-Positioning Paedophile Sellotape,' I replied.

Light-bulb moment. We both said, 'Wouldn't it be great if you could do something like the GPS tracker system for sex offenders?'

We talked for a while and realised we would need more than a computer program to track paedophiles live – the tracker themselves would need training and a back-up team to report any concerns.

From there, with the help of a good man called Clive Crosby, I developed ROM. It consists of an almost inde- structible bracelet worn round the ankle, which is connected to a GPS mobile phone, which is connected directly to the specially trained sex-offender management teams.

We spoke to a company called Benefon, who had already made GPS phones for loggers in faraway places that had emergency buttons that sent your coordinates and let people know you were in trouble. Until we got in touch with them, they had not yet explored offender tracking. Some months later, we'd worked up the ROM idea between us.

The bracelet would be linked to a phone, which would track the offender, linking them to a live tracking team, a 'spy in the sky', as all the papers called it at the time. Certain areas would be blocked to the offender, such as schools, parks and swimming pools, and if the offender entered one of their blocked areas, the GPS system would know and the offender's telephone would ring instantly, even if they were using their phone at the time.

In America, they loved the idea and now use this system. Here, though, it was a different story. Everything was going brilliantly. I spoke at a Labour Party Conference fringe meeting to introduce the system. I met and spoke with the then home secretary, Hilary Benn. I did loads of media and put the bracelet on a journalist, who tried to go near a blocked school and couldn't. We even tested it out on a Tory MP for a whole month, who said it was brilliant. When it came to conducting the proper government trials, however, they didn't use the full ROM package, meaning they tagged some offenders but not with our system. They never deployed the slaving ankle bracelet or other crucial elements to the whole ROM philosophy.

That's the way it goes sometimes though. ROM joined the other initiatives we continued to fight for, along with the cases we picked up along the way. It was too much for two people. We very shortly began to realise that we needed something more – more than just two people with their fingers in the dam. We had to do something about the dam. In the meantime, though, the cases kept coming in.

Part Two

Survivors

8

It was late one evening when the call came in about Pete Dawson. It must have been gone ten because I was interrupted watching *Family Guy* – one of my favourite shows – which is so rude and irreverent that they have to put it on late.

The call was from a detective based in the North. We'd met at a child-protection conference. He was a bit sheepish-sounding, full of apologies for phoning so late, saying he wouldn't have bothered us if he didn't think it was important, but that he had a problem.

'What's the victim's name?' I asked.

'Polly – Polly Dawson. Three-year-old at the family barbecue. The offender, Cook, was released on appeal.'

'Oh Christ,' I said, dragging myself away from *Family Guy* and making my way to the office, where I dropped into my chair in front of the computer, waggling my mouse to dismiss the screensaver and listening to the detective as he filled me in on the case and recent developments.

'We think Pete Dawson's going to go looking for Cook.'

'Who is Pete Dawson?' I asked.

'Polly's dad.'

I reached for my headset and plugged it in.

'We think Pete's going to do something stupid, Shy. We know he's made threats against Cook.'

'Well, *stop* him doing something stupid.'

'We've tried, but he knows it's us and he won't even pick up the phone. Listen, he's a good bloke, but he's hurting and I don't think us getting involved at this point is going to help matters, if you know what I mean.'

'Yeah,' I sighed. 'I know.'

As I spoke, I was trying to get Sara's attention. The Skype window on my PC's desktop showed me the view from Sara's webcam, an empty room yawning back at me. She was still awake or she would have shut her computer down. I tapped out an instant message and clicked send. She was probably halfway through making a cup of tea or something.

'Do you want us to speak to him, then?' I asked the detective.

'Could you?'

I paused, watching the Skype window, the view of Sara's empty room: a coffee cup, a stack of books and paperwork, a shirt on a hanger. All the familiar Sara chaos, but no Sara. Just a vacant chair.

Not without her I can't.

And then she was there, taking her seat, peering at her computer, seeing me and waving.

'Would you mind holding a moment?' I said to the detective.

I tapped out an instant message to Sara: *Gerald Cook – High Court appeal – just released on legal tec – 3-yr-old vic. Could you research immediately? Dad is on warpath right now*.

Sara leaned forward to type back, *Doing it now*.

'OK,' I said to the detective, 'let me have his number and leave it with us.'

'Thanks, Shy. Oh, and . . .'

'Yes.'

'Will you do it now? We think . . . Well, we think he could be . . .'

'Could be what?'

'What I'm saying is he could be close.'

'Close to what? To doing something?'

'Yeees.' He drew that word out.

'Where is he now?'

'That's just it. We don't know where he is, but we suspect he's looking for Cook.'

'OK,' I sighed. 'Don't worry – we'll do it straight away.'

'God, yes, please. We don't want Pete in jail. He doesn't deserve it, Shy. Not on account of Gerald bloody Cook.'

I pulled my headset off and started talking to Sara over Skype. 'Hello, treasure,' I said.

She smiled. 'Hi, hon. What have we got?'

I took a deep breath and filled her in.

One hot Sunday afternoon, Pete Dawson and his wife, Sheila, had had a barbecue. They had invited some neighbours and friends from work. The house had been full of people, including a couple not known to the Dawsons – some friends of friends. Gerald and Pauline Cook. In the evening, the guests had thinned out, leaving three or four couples behind, including the Cooks. All the children had gone home, apart from Polly of course, who lived there, and who had been floating around the way kids do.

Eventually the evening had wound down and the guests left. As they did so, Polly had pointed at Gerald Cook and told her mother, 'That man licked my front bottom.'

Imagine the shock – the way her words must have taken some moments to register. Initial disbelief. Embarrassment, even. Then the questions.

He'd done it twice, according to Polly. Once in the kitchen, then a second time in the bathroom, at which point he'd given her a pound coin.

Polly's parents had reported it, and her knickers had been analysed by police forensic scientists. Traces of saliva were found on the inside and outside of the underwear. The DNA had matched to that of Cook, who was arrested. After the trial, during which little Polly had had to give evidence, he had been imprisoned for three years.

But that wasn't the end of it.

Cook had appealed. His defence was that he had met Polly on the landing and picked her up because he wasn't sure whether she was able to use the stairs or not, at which point the three-year-old had touched his face, apparently slick with saliva, then jammed her hand down her knickers. Shocked, Cook had put her down, told her off for being naughty, said she was a 'bad girl', then given her a pound. As you do. The defence argued that little Polly was in a huff, having been told off by Cook. Because of this, she then invented the allegation that he had twice licked her 'front bottom'.

You couldn't make it up, could you? She was *three*. She couldn't even use stairs, according to the defence, remember. Yet they argued that she was capable of concocting a serious and damaging allegation of sexual assault so plausible it fooled her parents, the police and the original judge and jury. She'd even managed to work it so that the available DNA evidence would perfectly corroborate her accusations.

Sorry – I don't mean to sound flippant, but really. We weren't in court to see for ourselves, but did the defence really say this with a straight face? That a three-year-old had essentially concocted this whole story with all the expertise of a CSI detective?

Well, they must have done, because Gerald Cook won his appeal. Polly, having gone through the ordeal of giving evidence at the original trial, was 'ruled out' as a competent witness when the case came before the High Court and Cook's conviction was quashed.

We talk a lot about how the system fails victims. In many ways, our entire working life is spent trying to redress the balance, but there are some instances that leave even us speechless, some occasions that make you wonder, Are we on the same planet as these people? When a three-year-old girl's knickers are soaked in some vile bloke's DNA and he is acquitted.

When things like this happen, we chew it over for a while. Sometimes we even have a little cry. Then we dust ourselves off and get back in the ring. We try to change things so that maybe, just maybe, we can stop something like this from happening again.

We don't recommend anyone takes the law into their own hands. Every now and then, though, we encounter people who want to do just that. Pete Dawson, for instance.

When your child is abused, both mums and dads suffer terribly, but somehow with dads it's different. Every father of every child abused by the Gerald Cooks of this world says, 'I'm gonna get 'im.' He'll tell you in great detail exactly what he'll do if he ever catches up with him – right down to the squishy sound that his fingernails will make when he extracts them with a pair of pliers. To know that his little one had been sexually abused, that he wasn't there to do anything about it, that he couldn't make it right, is one of the most emasculating things that can happen to any father.

So what do they do? They pledge revenge. They might even take steps towards actually *taking* revenge: buy a baseball bat, talk to a guy who knows a guy in the pub. But here's the thing – we know this, and the police know this – they hardly ever go through with it. This is because even through their veil of grief and anger, they know their kids won't thank them for getting locked up. Perhaps they also know that deep down they're just a normal dad and there's a massive difference between plotting revenge and actually swinging the bat.

But what if the dad isn't a normal dad? He's one of the 'old school', let's say. A bloke you know is more than capable of swinging the bat, the kind the police start to worry about when they can't get hold of him.

Which is where we were now.

'Bloody hell,' said Sara, when I'd finished.

'OK,' I told her, 'I'd better ring him now.'

'Good luck. I'll look online and see what I can find,' she said, as she bent towards the keyboard, beginning research.

This guy would be emotional, highly strung, volatile even. He'd be quoting that appeal at me, so we needed the facts at hand. Usually, we have a team of online experts and people we call 'web ferrets' to rely on if we can't find what we're looking for, but that night we were on our own.

I left the Skype talk open, so Sara could hear the conversation – my end of it at least. It's not ideal that Sara can't hear the other end of the conversation, not when we're working together, but then nobody's going to benefit from a three-way conversation in a situation like this: you can't do talk-down on a conference call. Instead, what we'll do is communicate by Skype or shrugs and gestures and even through sign language.

You may remember from my book *Broken* that I was beaten so badly I lost my hearing for a time. During this period, I learned sign language and it's a skill I've kept up. I ended up passing some on to Sara and some of the long hours we spent in the early days of our friendship involved me teaching her sign language over the webcam. It often comes in handy. At times like this, for example, when we need to talk without speaking.

I called the number.

'Yeah,' said a voice. More like a growl, really. Like the sound you might expect from a bear if you surprised it during dinner.

'Is that Pete?' I said.

'Yeah,' he growled dangerously.

'Hello, Pete. It's Shy Keenan here. Are you all right, darlin'? I hear things aren't so good your end.'

There was a pause. 'Bloody hell. I can't believe you phoned me.' The growl softened.

He seemed to know who I was. My reputation preceded me. Great – it meant I didn't have to establish our credentials. Sara was looking at me with eyebrows raised. In return I gave her a thumbs-up.

'I understand you've been through the mill lately,' I said to Pete. 'Do you want to tell me what's happening?'

'You don't want to know,' he replied slowly. 'You do *not* want to know.'

I said, 'Well, I've called you, so I absolutely do want to know.'

He laughed and I knew right then I had him. I knew I could deal with this guy.

Another thumbs-up to Sara. She grinned back. An instant message flicked up: *Can you reach him?*

I think so, I keyed.

She nodded.

'So what's up?' I said to Pete.

'You know where I am, don't you?' he said. 'You know what I'm doing, don't you?'

'Not really. I was hoping you could tell me.'

'No, Shy, no.' His voice dipped. 'I can't tell you. Not you.'

'OK, look,' I said, 'before we go any further, I need you to promise me one thing.'

'What's that?'

'I need you to promise me that before you do anything, you'll give me a chance to talk. Just talk. That's all.'

'It won't change anything, Shy,' he said.

'Well, then, it won't hurt to talk, will it?'

'Fair enough,' he said.

'You promise?'

'Promise.'

'OK, then, why don't you fill me in on what's happened?' I said.

I already knew the salient details of the appeal, of course – I still had the bruise from where my jaw had hit the floor – but I needed to hear it from Pete.

And, very quietly, he said, 'Conviction quashed.'

'I know, Pete, I heard, and—'

'Con-vic-tion quashed.' Slightly louder now.

'Pete—'

'Conviction. Fucking. Quashed.' Now he was shouting, really shouting.

'OK, Pete, you've got to calm down for me. I've already been deaf once. Calm down, sweetheart. I can't hear you properly. I need to hear you to help you. First, tell me where you are.'

'I'm outside his house.'

Oh, no. 'Say that again for me, Pete. I'm not sure I heard you right.'

'I'm outside his house, Shy, and in a minute I'll be inside his house. He is *this close* to going to Hell. I've got a fucking bat here an' all. I'm going in there, Shy.'

In sign language I told Sara, *He's outside the house.*

An instant message came back: *What house?*

I typed, *I think Cook's house.*

In sign language she came back: *Oh crap.*

'Right,' I said carefully. 'And is he in there, Pete?'

'Oh, he's in there.'

'Come on, how do you know?'

'I can see him. I can see the back of his head. He's watching the news.'

Great.

An instant message from Sara: *Got judgment. Reading*

now. She'd been on to the High Court's website to check the details.

'Pete, are you alone?' I said.

'I've got a mate with me in the van.'

Talking to him, I felt like I'd been plunged into an emotional war zone. People's lives were at stake here. This wasn't a normal dad doing his bit to satisfy his rage. This was Pete, who was clearly more than capable of swinging that bat.

I tried to imagine him staring at the back of someone's head. Gerald Cook's head? I had no idea. I just knew I couldn't let him go in there. That was it. That was our priority. Stop Pete from going in there.

'Pete,' I said, 'do me a favour? I'm afraid I've got to visit the little girls' room. I'll be straight back, all right?'

'Right, Shy, right.' He coughed a little, probably a bit embarrassed because I'd said something about needing the loo. Men are so funny like that.

'You hang on there. You promise, all right?'

He promised.

I silenced the connection. Seconds later, Skype bleeped and I was talking to Sara.

'Is he outside the house?' she said.

'Yes.'

'Shit, Shy, what's he planning?'

'To go in there, and, I quote, "Send him to Hell."'

'All right. Well, I've scanned the appeal and it's pretty tight.'

'How tight?'

'Well, the family have been shafted.'

'So is there anything to come back on it legally?'

'Don't reckon.'

'Bugger.' I took a deep breath. 'What do we do now?'

'Get back in touch with the copper. Tell him what's up.'

'Risky. We don't want Pete up for intent.'

'True, but look at the alternative. No way do we want him doing life for the likes of Gerald Cook. Maybe we could get the police to send a patrol car round there. Something to scare Pete off for the time being.'

Not for the first time, I thought, Jesus, she's incredible. She'd have every right to be cheering Pete on. Somehow, though, against all the odds, she sees past her own emotions, and she does it day in, day out. Whatever she's on, I wish I could get some.

Right, I was thinking. Pete's a bloke and blokes have entrenched ideas about women in the toilet, so I've got at least five minutes before he begins to wonder if I've fallen in. I punched in the number for my detective, praying he'd answer the phone.

He didn't. I got a colleague instead, so I went through it with him, omitting certain details, giving him plenty of 'I have reason to believe', 'Potential breach of the peace' and 'Better safe than sorry' stuff. I asked him to send a car round to check on Cook right now and rang off.

Back to Pete, who was still there, thank God – still staring at the back of Cook's head, who remained watching the news, oblivious to the fact that he was moments away from making an appearance on it.

It soon became clear that Pete had wound himself up even more during my fake toilet break. Now he was ranting.

I was hearing things about journeys to Hell, bastard justice, DNA evidence and dickhead lawyers. Bad, bad stuff.

To Sara I typed, *Listen to this*.

Then to Pete, I said, 'Hang on, I'm just going to put you on speakerphone while I light a cigarette.'

I let Sara hear him on the speaker. Enough for her to get an idea of his mood, of what we were dealing with. She winced and typed out an instant message: *We need to calm him down*.

I nodded. 'Pete?' I said.

'Yeah.'

'Don't suppose I could have a word with your mate there, could I?'

I could hear him passing me over.

'Hello.' Another growly voice.

'Hello, Pete's mate,' I said brightly.

'You all right, Shy?'

'Oh, I'm just fine, thanks, sweetheart. Tell me, what's your name?'

'James.'

'Any chance of talking him out of this, James?'

'I'm here for Pete, Shy – driving for him and that. I'll do whatever he wants. Cook's a piece of dirt. He don't belong on the earth, if you know what I mean.'

I signed to Sara something that broadly translated as *Damn – no help there, then*.

'You're his mate, James. What calms him down?' I asked.

'A drink, normally.'

'All right. How about you do me a favour, darlin'. Do you have an offy nearby?'

'There's one not far away, yeah.'

'Then go get him some booze, eh? Do that for me. So I can have a good talk with him. I just need to calm him down a bit. Do it for me, please. Do it for Pete. For little Polly.'

Yes, yes, I know – it was a cheap shot, but they clearly cared about Polly and I was willing to try anything.

There was a long pause. Sara and I looked at each other doubtfully.

'OK, Shy, will do.'

I breathed a sigh of relief, heard him pass the phone back to Pete, then the sound of the van door opening and closing.

Help is on its way, I kept telling myself. Help is on its way. And it couldn't arrive soon enough, because once again I could hear the emotion rising in Pete's voice. Moments after we started talking again, Pete was shouting, even more loudly than before.

'I've dealt with my affairs, Shy. I'm ready to do my time.'

'You're ready to do your time, are you?' I shouted back, startling both him and Sara. 'Well, that's good. What about Polly? Is she ready for you to do your time? You want Polly coming to the visitors' centre, do you? You want that? Because we both know it's not exactly a sunny day out at Alton Towers, is it? It's noisy and it's nasty and you wouldn't put someone you love through that kind of crap, would you?'

'He don't deserve to live, Shy.'

'And Polly, what does she deserve? What about her, eh?'

'I'm gonna kill him,' he roared, 'and I just want you lot to know that I'm doing it because of what he did to my baby. I don't want people saying I'm just a murderer. This is just justice being properly served.'

Then I heard the van door open and close, and it clearly wasn't James getting back inside. I wasn't getting through to him.

'Pete . . .'

My senses went to red alert, translating the tiniest sounds into images, hearing his feet hitting the hard pavement.

'Pete!' I shouted.

I could hear his breathing, fast and short, and then a *click-click*. What the bloody hell was that?

'Pete!' I screamed. 'Get back in the fucking van. *Right now.*'

9

The footsteps stopped.

'Please just let me talk to you,' I yelled, sounding more forceful than I felt. 'You promised me. What is five minutes? Just let me talk to you. You promised me.'

I could hear his breathing. I could virtually hear him struggling to make the decision, and I was praying he'd make the right one. Where the bloody hell were the police? And where was James with the booze?

'How did you know I was out of the van?'

'Woman's intuition. Get back in the van now. Just let us talk.'

I heard him get back inside, the solid *thunk* of the door shutting. I didn't give him a second to relax before laying into him. I gave it to him both barrels. 'Are you sure that once you've done this, you will have got them all?'

'What? What you talking about?'

'Well, when you kill this one, this one paedophile, and you're in jail, will you be absolutely sure you've got them all, so none of the others can touch her? Because in truth, there's loads more out there than Cook, so if you're in jail, what are you doing? You're just giving her up to them.'

He began to cry – not a normal cry, but a deep, guttural, angry cry, yelling about DNA and the police and paedophiles who don't deserve to live.

Christ, I thought, this isn't going to work. I've got two options here: either I phone the police back, get honest on their ass and risk Pete getting done, or I get him to speak to Sara. Sara's my ace in the hole, because whatever kind of a day you're having, it's not as bad as Sara's best day, so get over it. She doesn't ever say that, of course. She doesn't give off even the tiniest hint of being broken, but it's that effect she has on people.

She gets strange looks in shops. Anywhere, actually, that she goes. More often than not it's the 'Don't I know you?' look from people who recognise her but can't place her. Sometimes they'll talk to her. They'll be halfway through the 'Don't I know you from somewhere?' and you'll see the colour drain from their face as it suddenly dawns on them why they recognise her. What *do* you say to Sara, after all? But Sara is always very good with them. She'll smile and put them at ease.

Others know who she is straight away, but recognise her not as Sara . . .

'Are you Sarah's mum?'

'Yes,' she tells them, with a warm smile. 'Yes, I am.'

If you ask Sara how many children she has, she says, 'Five.' Sarah's always with her. Even if it's not in this realm. She doesn't, as many may expect, think of her baby daughter as a murdered child; she sees her as the lively, vivacious child she knew, loved and misses. More than that, Sarah's always with her because it's in her name that Sara does what she does.

'Do you mind at all,' I asked her once, 'people coming up to you?'

'Not at all,' she said. 'I never mind it. It's lovely because it means that they've remembered her, which is amazing. It was always so important to me that she wouldn't be forgotten, and she hasn't been. She's Sarah and she's rocking the world. She's changing the way people deal with sex offenders, the way people think and talk about sex offenders. Far from remembering her for how she died, they know her better for the positive changes she represents since she died. I'm proud of that. Maybe that seems like a strange thing to say, but that's the way that my brain handles it all.

'Sometimes I get people trying to tell me their story, which can get difficult, especially if they stop me in the middle of a crowded street. But I think that for the most part people just want to let me know that they've recognised me and that they remember Sarah, and I think that's lovely.'

Very often when people call and speak to me, Sara will send her love and best wishes, and they are always touched down to their toenails that Sara even knows about them, let alone cares how they are feeling. She has such a calming effect. She really means something to people.

That night, she was my secret weapon, though I didn't feel I needed her yet.

James arrived back. I heard cans popping, and for a while Pete and I talked, just talked. I let him drink, hoping it would calm him down, tapping out messages to Sara at the same time.

Sara then came up with a piece of genius. *Suggest he's got the wrong house*, she wrote in a message, raising her eyebrows at the same time, as though to say, 'It might work – you never know.' This was a very real concern.

After all, the police I'd asked for clearly hadn't turned up at this address, so either Pete was at the wrong house or the police were.

When he'd finished the cans, Pete laid into some Scotch. After a while, he was just rambling, calmer but rambling all the same.

'OK,' I said to him, trying to change the tone, 'I have a question for you.'

Pete said, 'What's that?'

'How many paedophiles does it take to wallpaper a living room?'

'I don't know, Shy. How many paedophiles does it take to wallpaper a living room?'

'Depends on how thinly you slice them.'

He barked with laughter. 'Oh my God, I've just blown Scotch out me nose.'

Sara was making groaning faces on the screen in front of me. She'd heard them all before.

'Another question. What do you give a paedophile who has everything?' I asked.

'I don't know, Shy.'

I said, 'A bigger parish.'

Got him again.

Still he was muttering about putting Cook in Hell, how he was a piece of dirt who deserved to die and that justice had failed his baby girl. Once again I found myself reminding him of Polly.

'What have you done to me?' he wailed. 'One minute I've got Scotch coming out me nose, the next I'm crying like a baby.'

'Careful or I'll tell you another joke.'

He giggled.

At last he was sloshed enough for James to take him home. The next morning, Sara and I got together and I spoke to him for about four hours. He was still pledging to go back and get Cook, but he'd simmered down a little. He was back to normal-dad levels, talking about it, fantasising about it, but unlikely to see it through.

Later the next day, I spoke to my detective, who filled me in on Pete's physical proportions. Turns out he's well over six foot up, down and across, with muscles on his muscles and a temper like ten angry men. I almost laughed down the phone recalling the scene from the previous night – me, five foot three, shrieking, 'Get back in the fucking van,' at him. There can't be many who can speak to Pete like that and walk away unscathed.

'Shy, you're a bloody nutter,' laughed Sara.

Yeah, you and me both, girl.

Sara and I worked on that case for weeks and I spent over twenty hours on the phone to Pete in the end. Sometimes he'd go back to the brink and I'd pull him back, saying, 'You go away for fifteen years, that's not protecting your little girl, is it? You can't protect her from anything in prison, can you? You think she's going to be dead proud of her daddy when he's doing a stretch for murder? When she's older, she may end up saying, "You weren't exactly there for me, though, were you, Daddy?"'

Another time, I told him, 'Do you know what, Pete? I wish I'd had a dad like you. I wish I'd had a dad who cared about me the way you care about Polly. But you'd be no good to me in jail. I would have needed you to stay with me. You would have protected me and made me feel safe.' I wasn't lying either. I meant every word.

I told him we'd look into the appeal. 'If you give us just three weeks and I look into this and nothing happens, what's changed? Nothing. All I need is three weeks. If there's nothing we can legally do, I won't argue with you about where you park.'

I knew full well, I would, of course, though thankfully it never came to that.

In the end, there was nothing we could do with the High Court judgment, as this is the highest court in the land. Cook's conviction was quashed and he was free to go.

We did, however, stop Pete that night, for Polly's sake. Sadly, not long after this, his family split up. It usually does. Something like that is like a bomb going off in the middle of a family and can rip it apart.

Pete didn't do time, though, that was thing – he could still be there for his daughter. We keep a special Phoenix box for little Polly, which is a wooden box containing a medal in recognition of being brave enough to tell. After all, that is in part what being a Phoenix is all about.

IO

Not long after this, Sara and I received one of the most disturbing emails we had ever come across.

> Dear Shy and Sahra we are alone i cant say whats been hapening i dont know how to its been hapening since i was born i think. we will both die if i talk to anyone just like the other one and i will be sent to jail for everything that hapened. i now everything is wrong i'm older now i don't want to speak about me but i want to save the baby i can't eat, sleep or deal just thinking about whots happening it's disgusting and wrong i don't know how to stop it i dont want to go to jail its just to bad and im so scared the baby will die if i tell and i will proberbly be next, because accidents will happen how can i save the baby can you help us please.

We sometimes get people sending us vague or coded messages, and we're on the receiving end of the occasional hoax. Was this a wind-up or a genuine cry for help?

Difficult to tell.

We tried reply-to-sender, but the email bounced back.

A joke, then. A sick joke.

But no. There was something about this message that made us think twice. Those words that chilled the blood:

'we will both die if i talk to anyone just like the other one.'

'What do you think, Sar?'

'God, where do you start? I'm worried about the baby, but it's hard to tell if the writer is a boy or a girl, a child or an adult, the abuser or even a murderer. What do you reckon?'

'I don't think it's an abuser. I know victim-speak and I feel like I recognise the language here. Most offenders don't normally care about what happens to any child, but this person seems to care. Adult or kid? Well, it's what they are not saying that gets me thinking. It's very guarded, so much so it makes me think it's not a child. Plus, they've contacted us through the website, so they clearly have some grown-up skills.'

We talked around it for hours, deciding in the end to put a message on our site. Hopefully our mystery correspondent would see it and get back in touch. We got our web ferrets on the case to see if the email address appeared elsewhere online. They promised to look into it. Then we did the only thing we could do, which was to wait. Cross our fingers and wait.

In the meantime, we had one of our most serious cases to deal with, involving an abuser named Wood and his victim, Libby – a very brave little girl we call Little Miss Phoenix.

11

Wood was a convicted sex offender who had served time for sexually abusing a child. He was released from jail and moved to a probation hostel, which housed a significantly high number of sex offenders. It wasn't a sex offenders' hostel as such – there was no sign on the door to say so – it just had a lot of sex offenders in it. Strange, then, that it wasn't a monitored hostel; in other words, there was no member of staff overseeing who came and went.

One night, Wood and a friend, Darren, went for a drive. It is alleged that while they were out, they tried to lure two children into their car, a pair of girls, who told their parents what had happened. The police were informed. For whatever reason, this was not traced back to the hostel or to Wood and his mate, and so they went out the next evening, again in a car, only this time to somewhere Wood knew.

He and Darren drove to the home of Fiona Burns, who was at home with her husband, Tom, and their three-year-old daughter, Libby. The two were strangers to each other, connected only by a loose acquaintance to a distant friend of the family who lived not far from Fiona and Tom. This loose historical friendship was back before Wood (unbeknownst to Tom and Fiona) first went to prison, and the Wood family had moved since. All that Wood really knew about Fiona was that she vaguely knew his mum, lived nearby and had a young daughter. Fiona only vaguely recognised Wood.

That night, he and his mate drove round to see if Fiona still lived at the house Wood remembered: a normal, non-descript house in a terrace on the outskirts of a large city. They pulled up in the road outside the house, went to the front door and knocked.

It was about 10.20 p.m., a cold night, when Fiona answered to find Wood and Darren on the doorstep. She was thinking, what's this guy doing knocking on my door? She wasn't happy, so as they talked on the doorstep, she very quickly introduced into the conversation the fact that Tom was at home. Even so, the pair didn't seem fazed and somehow managed to talk their way into the house.

Once inside, they moved through the hall and past the stairs. Libby was quietly playing on the upstairs landing, just outside her bedroom, and refusing to be sleepy. Libby was a sweet, active, fun-loving three-year-old and a big Mr Men fan.

Fiona and Tom exchanged uncomfortable glances, and Fiona moved to put the kettle on. They chatted for a moment or so, before Wood took advantage of a brief distraction by Darren to slip down the hall out of sight of Tom and Fiona. After a few moments, when he didn't immediately reappear, Tom called out Wood's name.

No answer.

Tom went to investigate and saw the front door was open. He called again, 'Hello? Mate? Are you there?'

No answer.

A worm of disquiet entered Tom's stomach.

'Mate?'

No answer.

'Libby?'

Silence.

'Libby!'

Tom turned. He looked through the front door and noticed that Wood's car was no longer parked outside the front of his house. In that moment, a terrifying realisation swept over him. He heard Fiona running from the kitchen to the front door, having sensed something wrong from the note of panic in Tom's voice. She was almost knocked sideways as Darren tried to dart past her to get to the front door and escape.

Tom came at him, face contorted, as he screamed, 'Where is she? *Where is she?*'

But Darren wouldn't say. He claimed he didn't know.

What had happened was that Woods had spotted Libby at the top of the stairs as he walked into the house. At the very first opportunity, while Darren distracted the parents, Wood had stepped away out of the parents' line of sight, scooped up Libby, let himself out through the front door, bundled her into his car and driven off to the hostel, a twenty-minute drive away.

Back at the house, Tom had Darren captive. He hauled him into his own car to go in pursuit of Wood and flagged down a police car. The officer took custody of Darren.

Having taken Darren's details and extracted from him information about Wood and the hostel, the police officer gave Darren a lift to his stepfather's house, not far away, and left him there. The officer then simply called in the information and went about his business. Beggars belief, doesn't it?

Only fifteen minutes had elapsed between when Libby was abducted to when Tom handed Darren over to the police.

Wood sexually abused Libby on the way to the hostel. Once at the hostel, he took her to his room. When he'd finished, it is alleged that he shared her with others.

Once Darren was at his stepfather's house, he lost no time in getting a lift back to the hostel to warn Wood that the police were after him. Wood took Libby and once again bundled her into his car. By the time the police eventually arrived at the hostel – over an hour and forty minutes after the first 999 call – Wood had already left the hostel with Libby. They had missed him by a matter of minutes. This time they did at least arrest Darren.

Meanwhile, Wood was driving around in his car. Occasionally he'd park to sexually abuse Libby again. Then, at about 2.30 a.m., in a different county, he went through a red light – with no headlights into the bargain – and was spotted by the local police.

A pursuit was initiated. The officers in this car had no idea he had a child with him, let alone an abducted one, so when Woods refused to stop, they began pursuing him at speeds of over 100 miles per hour. The chase ended when, at high speed, Wood appeared to purposely crash the car, completely writing it off. Later, in court, Wood claimed that he had tossed Libby from the open window of the speeding car in order to try and save her life. Nobody believes that for a second. Most people believe that he was trying to throw her out in some vain attempt to eject or wipe out 'the evidence' of his terrible crimes against her.

Thanks to sheer luck, she somehow survived. As a result of the crash, the road took a lot of her skin off. She had a severe case of road rash from head to toe and some big bumps and bruises, but by some miracle she had sustained no broken bones and was taken to hospital. In total her ordeal had lasted just over four hours.

In hospital, she was given an external 'rape-kit' examination, which looked for injury and tested for any DNA evidence or sexually transmitted diseases. She was treated and sent home the very next day. No one had even talked to her or her family about what had happened or given them any advice on who to turn to for help and support. This was just the latest in a series of ghastly failures on the part of the authorities involved in this awful case.

Those failures kept on coming. Over the following days, weeks and months, Libby told her parents about some of what had happened to her. She says it in her own words, but she basically says she suffered every kind of sex crime imaginable at the hands of more than one person during her time in the hostel and in the car after leaving the hostel. Nobody from anywhere ever asked the family if they were all right or in need of any help; nobody spoke to Libby about what had happened to her or asked if she was all right; unbelievably, despite the fact that Wood was jailed for what he did to her and the fact that she has shown that she wants to talk about it, to this day no one in authority has ever asked Libby about what happened to her or how she is.

Tom and Fiona were later told that a force helicopter had been involved in the chase, but the police have never revealed any footage recorded by either the police cars or a helicopter.

Wood was charged and jailed for kidnapping, three counts of sexual assault and drink-driving. He was given a five-year tariff on his life sentence, which was not increased on appeal. His accomplice, Darren, was never charged with anything.

If the police had triggered their own child-abduction protocol, things could have been so different. If the police had properly investigated each of the crimes committed in this case, all of those responsible for what happened would have been held accountable.

These days, for Libby, our Little Miss Phoenix, the terrors mainly come at night. She screams in her sleep. Fiona and Tom, distraught and helpless, were forced to hear their little girl's night-terror screams and would just sob. As if that wasn't enough to deal with, they were further tortured by the fact that she had been so severely let down by the authorities, whose job it was to protect her, help her and get her some justice.

Libby's case is what we call a 'catastrophic system failure'. This is where every part of the system that is meant to act fails in some way to take the proper action. It is rare, but when it happens, as the term suggests, it can have catastrophic consequences. There were issues here from start to finish with the probation service, who let Woods stay at such a hostel unsupervised, all the way through to the judicial process and beyond – failures that just defy all reason and common sense.

Tom and Fiona contacted us and we helped the family launch the barrow load of complaints to all the many different departments attached to these failing services. After years of investigations, they finally admitted that they had indeed collectively failed Libby and they publicly apologised to her and her family.

Libby's parents wanted to do more than just complain, though; they wanted to achieve something useful for future victims of this sort of crime; they wanted to achieve something they wished they had had when Libby was abducted; they wanted their police force to have an active Child Rescue Alert system, which was the UK's version of the very famous Amber Alert.

12

Tosh, or, as he's more formally known, Chief Inspector Martyn Underhill, works with Sussex Police. During the period between when Sarah disappeared and Whiting was convicted for her murder, Tosh was one of Sara's closest confidants and he went on to become one of her dearest friends. He has a reputation for not having a single unsolved case on his books. He is often brought in on the most high-profile cases and to train other police officers in his field. He and Sara frequently work together, to train other family-liaison officers. After Tosh heard about Amber Alert, he was asked to do some research into it, to find out whether it was feasible for the UK.

Amber Alert is an American initiative. It's short for 'America's Missing: Broadcasting Emergency Response', but is also named after a child, Amber Hagerman, a nine-year-old girl who was kidnapped and murdered in Texas.

It was 13 January 1996. Amber and her brother, Ricky, had asked their grandparents if they could go for a quick ride on their bikes and were told they could, but just once round the block. They pedalled a short distance to the parking lot of a former Winn-Dixie supermarket that had been closed for some time, but where local kids enjoyed riding on a ramp. None more so than Amber and her brother, who played there for a while before Ricky said he was going home. Once there, he was asked where Amber was. Ricky said she'd stayed to ride on the ramp and he was sent back to fetch her. He returned moments later. Alone.

The children's grandpa drove to the parking lot. He spotted a police car and pulled up to it. The officer told him that a man who lived nearby had heard screaming and seen a man carrying a girl into a pickup truck. The witness had called 911 and the officer had raced to the scene, but all he had found was a bicycle. Only eight minutes had passed from when Amber rode away on her bike to when the 911 call was made.

Four days after her abduction, a man walking his dog found Amber's body in a creek bed. An autopsy showed that she had been kept alive for two days before she was killed. To date, no one has been convicted of her murder.

After campaigning by Amber's parents, the first Amber Alert trial was run in 1996, and by 2002, twenty-six states had signed up to it. Simply put, when a child under seventeen goes missing and there is evidence to prove that they have been abducted, a public-information alert is triggered, which means the general public will be alerted via the media, text messages, signs on motorways and in stores, and it will be done with the same level of urgency expected of a severe weather warning.

It works, and after seeing the benefits of such a system, Tosh and his colleague DCSI Jeremy Paine worked to bring something similar to the UK. As a result, Child Rescue Alert was born. By the beginning of 2002, Child Rescue Alert was introduced in Sussex as a trial. By the end of 2002, Tosh was pushing for it to go national. At first, uptake was slow. There seemed to be a reluctance to pay to set up a system that police felt they would rarely use, because to be fair to them, they probably deal with one or two kidnappings a year. Contrary to popular belief, paedophiles rarely kidnap kids. Therfore, to put it crudely, forces might well decide they have other things to spend their money on. But in the States, Amber Alert has saved lives. Thanks to Amber Alert, nearly 400 children have been recovered since 2003 – 80 per cent in the crucial first seventy-two hours.

Like Amber, the Child Rescue Alert is all about assessing risk. If a missing person is identified as being 'high risk', the media are told, local news broadcasts will be made, and the police will be on high alert. Police officers are required to make a judgement on whether or not to trigger the process. The first question asked is, why has the child been abducted? If the police go to the parents' house and find themselves driving up a sweeping gravel approach to a stately home, where a butler answers the door, then there's a possibility the child's been abducted for financial reasons. In Fiona and Tom's situation, it would have been clear to police that the abduction of Libby was not triggered by money. While they are not poor exactly, if you were going to choose a family to blackmail, you'd probably go to the other side of town. The second question asked is whether there is a possibility that this is a domestic dispute. Again, this was clearly not the case for Fiona and Tom. They were not a couple at war, and there was nothing to suggest that Libby might have been taken as part of a domestic dispute. Police had a description of Wood and the car he was driving. For the policeman arriving at the scene that day, the decision to activate the Child Rescue Alert should have been a no-brainer – every single criterion was satisfied.

Fiona and Tom's local police force were signed up to Child Rescue Alert. They *should* have used it, but they didn't. It's our firm belief that if the Child Rescue Alert had been triggered that night, a great deal of the abuse that Libby endured would have been avoided. It's even possible that the attacks at the hostel could have been prevented altogether. If it had been activated, then the police chasing Wood would have known that Libby was in the car and the pursuit would have happened according to a different set of rules. You don't chase a car at high speeds when you know there's an infant inside. Both of the policemen in the car that chased Wood were broken up about it. Both fathers, it broke their hearts when they found out. They were furious that nobody had told them.

That's why to this day Sara and I keep banging on about Child Rescue Alert to any force that will listen. We meet high-ranking police officers and what we're telling them is this: Child Rescue Alert is expensive, it requires training, and you may never use it, but that one time you do, you'll be so glad you had it.

The same goes for the European Child Rescue Alert. Being comparatively good with our child-protection laws in the UK has a downside – we tend to export our paedophiles abroad to other poorer, less developed countries. With that in mind, Sara and I worked for some time to bring about a kind of European Child Rescue Alert team, but as always, traversing the very confusing European Parliament was like trying to jog in tar. What we wanted

– and we knew it wasn't going to be easy – was a team set up to alert the public when the worst happened, as well as an actual rescue team, helping to rescue children all over Europe.

That's what we wanted. There was a problem, though. Trying to track down MEPs, let alone lobby them, was like trying to knit smoke. Solving the Da Vinci Code would have been easier. But we had been working on it for some time and were slowly inching our way through it all. Then, in May 2007, just as we were discussing how we might make that next push in Europe, the horrifying news broke that little Madeleine McCann had disappeared.

What we saw unfold during the first five days of her disappearance reinforced to us the need for the European Child Rescue Alert team; it gave us the impetus to carry on knitting that European fog no matter how hard it got. Then, later on, when poor Maddie had been missing for months and months, we heard that Maddie's parents had visited Strasbourg and Washington to research Amber Alert and had called for the European Parliament to back an EU-wide missing-child alert system. They got the backing of at least 393 MEPs – just what they needed for the legislation to be considered. In doing what they did, they took 393 giant steps towards achieving a European Child Rescue Alert team.

13

What sort of human beings are they, anyway, these people who take children, who abuse them, who kill them, even? Who is capable of doing such terrible things to the most vulnerable? How do they come into your life?

There are about half a million known paedophiles in this country. Of those, only about 30,000 are on the Sex Offenders Register. A minority will themselves have been sexually abused as children, but many, many more admit to lying about having been abused, for mitigation and for sympathy.

On average each offender has upwards of six victims. If they are abusing a group or family of children, they will leave one child untouched, as a decoy in case they're caught. 'Well, ask her or him if I ever touched them. They'll tell you I didn't.'

They can be male or female, rich or poor, old or young. They come in all shapes, sizes, races, religions and professions. They're educated, uneducated, related, strangers, all kinds of people without exception. In short, there is no single unifying factor, other than that they are paedophiles – they sexually abuse or exploit male or female children under the legal age of consent. Even then, there are different types of paedophilia: infantophiles attack babies and infants; haebophiles normally attack pre-pubescent boys;

teenophiles attack male or female children aged thirteen to sixteen.

How do you spot one? You can't by sight. Oh, you might think you can. Most people believe that paedophiles have a look or a type, that they're all old, frightened loners. Unintelligent, greasy, ugly people who wouldn't dare say boo to an adult goose. Sure, that might be true of a few of them, the ugly mugs you see staring out at you from the pages of the *Sun*, for instance, but look at Gary Glitter (AKA Paul Gadd). Does he look frightened to you? No. The fact of the matter is that there is no physical type.

Their ability to hide in plain view, right under your nose, is one common trait, honed to a skill. In general, paedophiles are paedophiles first. Everything else they do will be done to facilitate their crimes, so they tend to be compulsive liars, manipulative social chameleons and masters at exploiting others' weaknesses.

A Phoenix once described them as a 'bag of poisonous tricks'. Their first trick is to try and convince you that 'They can't help what they do.' They can, of course. For the vast majority of paedophiles, there is no medical or physiological reason, no genetic excuse. They have nothing and no one to blame; as I said before, they do it simply because they want to and because they can.

They use fear, secrets, lies, guilt, death threats or the threat of suicide to groom their victims. They work on their own and in teams. They pit family against family and victim against victim. To keep them apart, yes, but also to keep them from talking to one another, from sharing the truth.

They often appear to have Pied Piper characteristics.

They use ploys to attract a child – anything from a rule-free house to free stuff, drugs, cigarettes, alcohol, money, special attention or freedom from punishment. Other Pied Piper elements are fame, popularity, wealth, access to or power in any kind of child amusement or sport.

By and large they get away with it because of the public's trust. They know the last thing you will ever assume is that they are a paedophile and that they're targeting your child. Paedophiles have noted and exploited the social breakdown of the traditional nuclear family over the last few decades: it has created a rich source of victims. Like most predators, paedophiles pick on the weakest first. The most obvious weakness to predators is a physical limp, but these predators can also identify emotional limps in both children and adults. They can see if your child looks neglected, but they can also tell if your child *feels* neglected. They have inbuilt radars and can sense low self-esteem and attack it with the speed of a shark.

They often do it with help. Most paedophiles have four or five male or female friends, or facilitators, in tow – some witting, some unwitting, but all very well groomed. They're needed because most paedophiles can't achieve or maintain a good social front; facilitators are used as a trusted go-between or someone to hide behind. All this so they can gain access to children.

Why? Why would you assist a paedophile? The answer often lies within the facilitator's own psyche. They seem to have some kind of emotional addiction to the paedophile's fantasy.

There simply isn't an organisation, industry, profession, religion or club that paedophiles have not or cannot infiltrate and exploit. The moment you think you are immune and conduct yourself with no offender identification or protection policy will be the moment you realise you are very likely to have a paedophile somewhere in your midst.

And what stops them? You would have thought, wouldn't you, that there were enough deterrents. The fact that if caught, they'll become a social pariah. Everyone will know. They'll be in the local press, maybe even the national newspapers if they've been particularly prolific or if they're a copper, vicar, comedian or pop star. Their friends will disown them; their own family will wonder what they have spawned. Somehow, though, they manage to shove all that to one side. Nothing gets in the way of their paedophile lifestyle. They'll wait and plan and plot and coax and coerce, over time, over weeks or months if necessary, to get what they want. And does it matter that what they want is illegal, immoral and carries with it the risk of imprisonment, pain and social shame? No, because they live in an almost permanent state of delusion. They've convinced themselves it's all OK, that it's everyone else who has got the problem.

Try and get your head round that. You can't, can you? That's why we say that you really need not try to understand the paedophiles' rhyme or reason – it's just a waste of your time, because if you do manage to get inside their heads, you won't see much you recognise. You certainly won't find empathy. You can't cause another living thing untold pain if you have empathy for them, you just can't. They're not like you and me. Try and look for bits of you in there and it'll be a fruitless search that can end up making you think that they must therefore be big, scary monsters. They're not monsters, though, or the bogeyman; they're cowardly and weak and prey on the vulnerable.

Yet somehow they can pretend to be as normal as the rest of us. Sure, in secret they have made the world's most repulsive life choices, but they can also pretend to behave perfectly normally.

If you start calling paedophiles 'monsters', they begin to sound all scary and tough and they are *anything* but. Remember, these are people who always pick on the smallest, weakest element in our families, our children, or the abandoned, the limping lambs in our society. Does that sound very tough and scary to you? Believe us, they're not. Believe me, I've met lots of them.

What they do have is their mask, and I guess that if there is anything scary about paedophiles, then it's that. It's the mask that allows them to appear to operate like normal people, like vicars or policemen or comedians or pop stars. It's a disguise made up of their denial, their secrets and their lies, a mask that because of my own childhood, I am more able to see.

'Shy?'

'Yeah?'

'We need your paedar.'

That's what Sara calls it – my 'paedar'. If it's on, then I'm looking for that deluded denial in someone, that mask. What else? I throw away my preconceptions for a start. Take Jonathan King. He's a loud, seriously deluded, arrogant attention-seeker, the exact opposite of how most people think of a paedophile – most people assume a paedophile has hollowed-out cheeks, wears an anorak and lives with his mother. Jonathan King, though, seems to be revelling in his status as an outsider, which is a common emotional trait among the most nefarious paedophiles. The way King stands up and proudly states what he's done, dismissing his child victims as nothing more than 'rent'. He's taken the facts and made them fit Jonathan King's world, a place where it's somehow OK to have sex with children, as long as you can find a suitable word to describe that process and his word is obviously 'rent'. Paedophiles do have some emotional traits in common: they're boundary-pushing control freaks with an absence of shame, empathy, respect and remorse – all the stuff that most normal people have.

You can, if you want to, spend endless hours on how they look or why they do it or even why they won't stop by themselves, but you'll be wasting your time. Alternatively, you can focus on how they do it, and do something more useful to get in their way. Empower yourself with knowledge about them and the law and you will have armed yourself as best you can against all but the most determined paedophiles. That said, it is important to note that no matter how much you learn and despite your very best parental efforts, you can still fall foul of the much rarer paedophile attacks suffered by Libby or indeed Sarah.

14

Our web ferrets came up empty-handed when they looked into that mystery email and we received no reply from the message we'd posted on our website. We'd talked to the police, who said there was nothing more they could do with so little information. Probably just an attention-seeking nut, they said, somebody trying to wind us up.

Then another one arrived.

> Dear Shy and Sara i saw you massage was it for me i cant believe it it was for me right i can't get emails they will now im not allowed out yet i don't go to school but i can use the email when they are out of it theres drugs i have to take to do it the babys ok right now I think nothing happens yet but it will hapen i now it will i dont want to die or make any one die again i want to save it if i can i now if i say no one will believe me i will go to jail if i have to but im scared they will hurt me whot happens if you tell is it bad will you still help me if im bad i don't now the words to say i will try get out and contact you from the liberary if you don't tell on me.

Again we couldn't respond to it.

'I'm worried big time,' said Sara, characteristically to the point. '"Not allowed out", "drugs", "die again" and "the baby"? What's happening here? A young girl being drugged who isn't allowed to go to school but is allowed to go to the library? Maybe she's home-schooled? Do you think the baby is hers?'

'I dunno. I don't think it's the way it seems. I'm not sure about the "die again" thing, and I don't think the baby is hers – a mother wouldn't call her child an "it", especially not one she cares this much about saving. And the drugs thing? I was drugged at one point, so I could be abused without a fight. Maybe that is what's happening here – it would explain the writing.'

'What do we do?'

'Well, *I* started pretending to take the drugs. That way, I could get my mind clear. Maybe we should tell her to do the same, so she can tell us more – we need more, like where is she from? Who does the baby belong to? Does she have family or teachers she can ask for help? Let's see if we can get her to write to us again. What do you think?'

'I say let's go for it.'

15

Bernadette Williams, or Berni to her friends, is a massive Elvis fan. She loves his music, his films and everything about him. She loves to collect Elvis memorabilia and liked to play his songs as she scrubbed her house to within an inch of its life.

She is a sweet, kind person who until April 2001 lived a quiet, ordinary kind of life – a single mum, bringing up her children, fussing over her pets and listening to Elvis. Her husband had walked out years ago, leaving her to it. She, her son and daughters lived in a nice house in Deptford, London. Deptford was a sort of council-bland, piss-smelling, scribbled-on area, but has recently, in the name of the upcoming Olympics, seen a makeover. Everything's had a lick of paint and it's looking a little better these days. Even so, the High Street was never full of big-name shops and still isn't. It has more than its fair share of small, boarded-up stores in between takeaways, off-licences, bargain carpet stores, arcades and pubs.

You grew up fast on these streets. If you weren't street-wise, you were victimised. So it was quite something to bring up good kids without them going down the gang-culture, criminal-record route. Berni was doing just fine with her three.

Her youngest daughter, Hannah, was a beautiful

fourteen-year-old girl, a friendly, trusting little soul, the apple of her mother's eye. She loved fashion and jewellery. She loved her music, mainly boy bands like Take That and Boyzone. She used to love singing and karaoke, and was really good at it. Berni remembers hours of fun lounging about on the living-room couch, listening to her daughter sing her favourite songs to her. 'I'm a Barbie girl in a Barbie world.' Strange how a song can make you smile and cry at the same time.

Hannah had some learning difficulties, particularly with reading and writing, but she was doing well at school and working hard to do better. She was a caring soul, popular. She loved her pets, and she loved her mum to bits.

Berni gave her a mobile phone so she would always know where Hannah was and who she was with. Hannah didn't mind. She never hung around with the 'dodgy crowd', anyway; she didn't behave the way they did. That made her mother proud. She'd use her phone to call home regularly, often just to catch up – to share a joke or gossip about who said what and why so-and-so wasn't talking to you-know-who.

She didn't seem that interested in boys. She had friends who were boys, who looked out for her, but her mum knew that change was just round the corner and she was ready to vet them. Berni was the same – careful with her friends. She'd had her heart broken and been betrayed, so she wasn't one to get carried away. She'd had one or two boyfriends over the years, but didn't really bring them into the family. She never wanted her children to grow up with one step-dad after another. She'd enjoy a boyfriend's company until it wasn't fun anymore and would then move on.

It was Saturday 21 April 2001 when Hannah went missing. It started out like any other day, different only because Hannah wanted to go shopping on the High Street and up to the local outdoor market. It was mid-morning. She told her mum she'd stay in touch and off she went, a day's shopping ahead of her.

As the morning wore on, Berni wondered why Hannah had not called as she usually did. At first, she didn't give it too much thought. Hannah would be busy having fun with her friends.

Later on, she'd still heard nothing, so Berni decided to give Hannah a call, just to check she was OK. Funny – her phone was switched off.

Oh well, thought Berni. Maybe she's in an area where the signal isn't so good. I'll call again in a little while, if she doesn't call me first.

She waited. Still no call. She tried Hannah's phone again, but it remained switched off. This was not like Hannah. A small, gnawing concern began to grow in Berni's mind.

Hannah was a good kid who stuck to the rules, but her learning difficulties made her just that little bit more vulnerable than other children her age. She was trusting, friendly. Sometimes *too* trusting and friendly. Berni was always aware that she would need to protect her child from those who would take advantage of that vulnerability.

As time went on, Berni tried the number a few more times but a message told her the phone was switched off. Now she was really beginning to worry.

The hours passed and it was starting to get late, dark even, and long past home time. Berni kept trying the phone and each time got that same message: 'I'm sorry, but the mobile you are calling is switched off. Please try again later.'

It just wasn't like Hannah to switch off her phone. She would normally never go this long without calling home. She would never stay out late without checking it was OK first. Never.

Berni called some of Hannah's friends. None of them had seen Hannah all day. Desperately trying to control a rising sense of panic, Berni called one last friend, one of Hannah's closest.

No, she said, she hadn't seen Hannah all day.

That did it. Berni and the friend took to the streets, frantically searching for Hannah. All to no avail.

Berni continued searching well into the small hours. With no sign of Hannah, she went to the police station to report her child missing. They took Hannah's details – what she looked like, what she was wearing – and listened as Berni explained that Hannah wasn't a runaway, that she was a vulnerable child, with learning difficulties. Then Berni rushed home to see if Hannah was there, with a broken phone, wondering what all the fuss was about.

The house was empty and an agonising dread started to seep into Berni's soul. All she could do was wait. To her, every minute seemed like a week. It felt like the whole world was on fast forward, while she was on a terrible, horror-stricken pause.

No sleep, no food. Just endless questions without answers, staring at the phone and the door, willing her to call, willing that door to fly open with her daughter bouncing through it bearing an explanation that would make it all better. Just endless hours of could haves, would haves, should haves; just pitiful pleas into the emptiness. Please bring her back.

Hours turned into days, days into weeks and the weeks into unbearable months. Berni would spend days and nights searching for her child. She managed to get the local college students to make up posters for her. She talked to anyone and everyone. She would hear through the grapevine that someone had seen Hannah, but instead of it filling her with hope, she'd scream inside: 'Why didn't they tell her that her mum was looking for her, that she loved her and missed her, that she was freaking out without her?'

It would hurt Berni to hear people say things like, 'Maybe she just ran away.' She knew they were trying to comfort her, but it wasn't comforting. She knew better than any other living soul that the only reason Hannah hadn't come home was because someone had stopped her from doing so.

It was the time of the very high-profile Milly Dowler and Danielle Jones cases. Two young girls who had disappeared off the face of the planet. Berni wondered why her child's case wasn't getting the same kind of attention. Not in a mean-spirited way, obviously. She just wanted her daughter to matter too.

Meanwhile, it seemed to her that the Met Police had all but written off Hannah as a runaway. They made a few local appeals, but never passed much information on to Berni. The more she pushed them about it, the more they appeared to lock her out.

'Do you know how many people go missing every day?' she was told.

'I couldn't believe what I was hearing,' she said later. 'I thought the police were here to help and protect us. I felt so completely alone. I didn't know what to do or say when people asked me, "What are the police doing?" I felt too ashamed to tell them that I just didn't know.'

Whenever Berni could sleep, which was rare and only for a few hours at a time, she had a recurring dream. In it her daughter was lost and stuck somewhere cold and unable to get home. It would leave her in pieces for days, so she tried not to sleep.

No matter what the police or anyone told her, Berni knew in her heart that Hannah was no runaway. She knew that she would never give up searching for her child till she found her.

What Berni didn't know, and didn't discover for nearly another year, was that Hannah had met a cruel and terrible man who had come into her life via an entirely unexpected route – and it was he who had taken her.

16

He was a violent paedophile called Robert Howard, later dubbed 'as evil as the Yorkshire Ripper' by police, and goodness knows, they weren't wrong. This was a creature who called himself 'the Wolf Man' and had a long, sickening catalogue of rapes and assaults behind him. He was a drifter, an alcoholic, quite bright by all accounts, over six foot tall and able to manipulate people, which is what he had done his whole miserable life.

Howard's first sexual conviction was in April 1965, for attempting intercourse with a six-year-old girl in London. He'd broken into the girl's bedroom, where he pretended to be a doctor and ordered her to undress. Then he performed various sexual acts upon her, injuring her in the process. During the attack, he urinated on her bed and in a drinking glass on her bedside table. He was captured after returning to the house a week later.

The investigating officer, Detective Inspector Barker, said, rather prophetically, that 'Howard is a dangerous individual. This was a particularly bad case of indecency. He is obviously capable of murdering a child.' Howard was sentenced to just *nine days* in Borstal. All this before his twenty-first birthday.

Four years later, Howard attempted to rape a young woman in the north-east of England. He had conned his

way into her home and tried to rape her, but she fought
back. She escaped and ran into the back garden, where
she was chased and knocked to the ground by Howard,
who then tried to strangle her. Neighbours were alerted
by screams. Howard ran away, but was eventually caught
and sentenced to six years in prison.

It is also alleged that later that same night, Howard
abducted a young woman at knifepoint, an eighteen-year-
old on her way home from work. He allegedly took her
into two separate buildings and kept her there for over
four hours while he raped and sexually abused her. It is
believed that the victim was too traumatised by the assault
to take any further action beyond the initial police statement.

In March 1974, Howard, presumably out before his full
term of six years was served, was jailed for another ten
years after being convicted of raping a fifty-eight-year-
old woman. Again, he had broken into her house. The
woman was gagged and bound with a sheet, then subjected
to a five-hour ordeal of sexual assault. She was also forced
to hand over her money to Howard. He served eight of
his ten years.

Between 1982 and 1993, Howard did not get caught for
any further sexual offences, but he was arrested, convicted
and given fifteen months in prison for larceny. He also
spent time at an alcohol rehabilitation unit in County
Down.

Then, in 1993, he lured a sixteen-year-old girl into his
flat in County Tyrone. The girl later told the court that
during a two-day ordeal, Howard drugged, stripped and
repeatedly raped her. Throughout, a noose was tied round

her neck. When she struggled, the rope was tightened and Howard threatened to kill her unless she did as he said. At last she managed to escape by breaking through an upstairs bathroom window.

During the subsequent hearing, Howard said the girl had consented. As a result, he was convicted of the lesser charge of unlawful carnal knowledge with the girl and was given a three-year sentence, which was, incredibly, suspended for five years.

Let's take a deep breath and perhaps read that last paragraph again. It was 1993 and having kept this poor girl prisoner for two days and done unspeakable things to her, Robert Howard was given a three-year sentence *suspended for five years*.

It gets worse.

In August 1994, while on bail for the rape of the sixteen-year-old girl, Howard offered Arlene Arkinson, a fifteen-year-old, a lift home. She disappeared and has never been found.

Though Howard was arrested and questioned about Arlene's disappearance, he wasn't charged at that time. Locals, believing Howard was the man responsible for the girl's death, or disappearance, hounded him out of Castlederg – they firebombed his home – and he moved to County Donegal, where he slept rough in a van. It was sometime around then that Howard held a woman in her twenties prisoner for several weeks. He beat and raped her. She became pregnant and gave birth to his only known child.

Howard was also investigated by the Garda, the Irish police, as a possible suspect for six missing girls and

women, whose cases formed the basis of an investigation
called Operation Trace. Howard's name was on a list of
sex offenders whose activities were of interest to police
during 1993 and 1998. Fiona Sinnott, Fiona Pender, Ciara
Breen, Annie McCarrick, Jo Jo Dullard and Deirdre Jacob
were all between seventeen and twenty-six years of age
and all disappeared during that time. The Garda, however,
found no concrete evidence linking Howard to the murders.

In March 1995, Howard moved to Scotland. There, he
was given a council house just yards from two schools.
(Yes, really, two schools.) Apparently, he was given the
house after telling officials he was a terrorist target. He
was later hounded out of the Drumchapel area of Glasgow
after a newspaper printed a story about his past.

This move led him to London, where he had a home
but also lived with his new girlfriend, Mary, and her child
in Kent. Mary was the ex-girlfriend of Berni's ex-husband,
Hannah's father. Hannah knew this woman and did not
view her as a stranger when she unwittingly introduced
her monster boyfriend, Howard, to her.

He bided his time.

17

Imagine the unimaginable. Your child is taken.

From the moment they're gone, everything changes. The world stands still, but at the same time moves on at an uncomfortable speed whether you're ready for it or not. You need all the help and support you can get, but you, your family, your extended family, your friends and neighbours, both current and historical, and everyone your child ever knew suddenly becomes a potential suspect.

At a time when you need their love and support the most, you are suddenly being forced to consider people you have loved and trusted your whole life with the darkest of suspicions. Did they do this? Could they have done this? Did they have motive or opportunity? Am I unwittingly being friendly towards my own child's abductor?

All of the time you are beating yourself up; your sleep-deprived brain is tortured with what ifs, should haves and if onlys.

And the questions. Oh dear God, the questions.

Where is my child? What is happening to my child? Who did this? Why did they do this? What has my child done to deserve this? When is my child coming home? When?

It never stops going over and over in your brain. You can't help but replay the last time that you had together and the last words that you spoke. You take some little comfort that you told them, like you always do, that you loved them more than anything in this world.

Everything is a massive contradiction. The house can be full of people yet seem so completely empty. Every sense is numbed yet at the same time on heightened alert. You need help and support but want people to stay the hell away from you. You want to talk but can't bear to say the words out loud. You want a hug but don't want to be touched. You want to die but you need to stay alive. You want to cry but you're frightened you'll never stop.

Whether you're religious or not, you suddenly find yourself talking to God. Well, not talking, more bartering, begging and pleading.

Please, please take me instead. Let it be some caring nut who just wanted a child of their own. Please, please let this one child be the one who comes home. I will do anything you ask of me, just let me see their face again and give them one more hug.

Every knock on the door or ring of the telephone makes your stomach churn and your heart ache as you wait to hear if any of your questions or your pleas will be answered. You want to know the truth, yet can't bear to hear it. So every time you open the door or answer the phone, you're willing it to be someone who is about to tell you that your child has been found safe and is on their way home, and when it's just another well-wisher, you can't hide your disappointment and just hope they will understand.

The first wave of the official invasion of every single part of your life, both private and public, is so hard to bear: they even take your blood and samples of your hair. Then comes the second, the invasion of your missing child's room, to glean every possible insight they can. They take away anything that bears their DNA. It's necessary, of course, but it still feels like an invasion.

Then comes the media invasion, both welcome and unwelcome, as they search for the exclusive unturned stones. Every inch of your life is viewed through a scope, just beyond that front door.

You want to escape all the well-meaning attention, the media and the police, and lock yourself in your child's room, just to feel near to them. You want to smell them, touch their things and hold them, but it's way too soon and it hurts too much, so you dash past their door and into your own room, just for a moment's peace and quiet. You need to put the world on pause, just for a little while, so you can try to take it all in and blank it out at the same time.

Ordinary life stands still – the cleaning, the cooking and the electricity bills. You can't go to work and you don't dare to leave the house. You want to be there to open the door and be the first face your baby sees as they come down the path, accompanied by the police.

You can't sleep properly. It's more like forced, short, unconscious gaps that you suddenly awake from. You hate sleeping because the waking is so hard – each time you come round, you are forced yet again to acknowledge the terrible reality that is now your horrible life.

There isn't a moment, not a single second, that your child is not on your mind. People can talk to you, have what they think are conversations with you, but most of it goes over your head. The only thing you can tune into is information about where your child could be, or what is being done to find them.

You do everything you can. They need a good likeness to put on the posters, to print in the papers, to show on TV, so you hand over a treasured picture that up until now was just another picture on the wall, along with all the other family members smiling back at you. You've walked past it a thousand times before, but now it means so much more.

You plead for help and information, telling people to search everywhere once, then search it again. Look everywhere you can think of and ask all of your friends. Any tiny piece of information, no matter how big or small, and even if you don't think it's important, please, please, please give the police a call.

The waiting is the hardest, most soul-destroying thing. You feel helpless, useless and frightened. You think about things you would never have considered before, like talking to a psychic or selling everything you own to raise a reward. You want the whole world to stop, to know, to care, to help you make it right. When it doesn't, you start to hate the world for getting on with life as if nothing has happened.

'It's not fair!' you cry inside. 'Stand still – don't you know what has just happened to my child?'

Then more waiting as your spirit starts to wilt, as the days turn into weeks and the weeks into months. You sometimes feel like you're the only one who cares, the only one who won't give up hope; that maybe, just maybe your child will somehow make it home, safe and sound, where they belong.

Then comes the dreaded knock on the door. It sounds exactly the same as it has always done, but somehow your instinct tells you this knock is different and you know that when you open it, you will be opening the door to a brand-new living hell.

You hesitate. Maybe you just won't open it. That way, it won't be real. Maybe you are wrong about the way you feel. Maybe they're not here to realise your worst fears. But that door will have to open and your soul will cry its tears.

'I'm so very sorry to tell you that we have found your missing child. It seems that they were murdered many months ago. There is little to identify, so we have checked through DNA. It's best you take back this picture now and try to remember them this way.'

'Please tell me you're mistaken,' you cry. 'Please say it isn't so.'

But your heart is breaking, because you know. You know.

Because of what has happened, there is no last look at their face, no last hug or kiss goodbye, not even a proper funeral – not until after the trial.

It is so hard to believe that a monster could take the life of such a sweet and innocent child, but it's true. Worst of all for you, until they are caught, found guilty and jailed and all their appeals give them no reprieve. Only then can the victim's family really start to grieve.

18

It was 15 March 2002 when Berni opened the door to the police. They had come to tell her that they had found a body and were at that very moment working on the identification. They told Berni that they thought it might be one of the other girls who had gone missing at that time – Danielle or Milly – and explained that they were waiting for the coroner before they could say for sure who it was.

Hannah had been missing for almost a year. During that time, Berni had never given up hope. She had maintained a poster campaign and constant searches in the hope of finding her daughter. She had refused to think the worst. Right up until that dreaded knock on her front door. Even now, she still allowed herself to hope that it wasn't Hannah who had been found.

As she closed the door on the police, the phone rang. It was her father. He said, in a voice that sent chills down her spine, 'Have you seen the news, sweetheart?'

'No,' said Berni. She hung up immediately, ran to the TV set. A friend in the house tried to stop her, but she switched it on – too scared to look and too scared not to – just as the news came on.

Her world fell apart.

As the newsreader described the clothes that the police

had found, Berni knew – because she had bought them for her child – that they were talking about her Hannah.

Her legs buckled, the breath went out of her. 'Oh, no,' she was saying, repeating it over and over. 'Oh, no. Oh, no. Oh, no. Not my baby. No.'

It felt like someone was ripping out her heart, like the lights were going out in every corner of her soul. An agonised, unspeakable groan rose from the deepest part of her body and just poured out of her.

As the newsreader continued to describe the crime scene, Berni tried not to picture her Hannah there. She tried so hard to hold on to that last image she had of her smiling daughter as she bounced out of the front door to go shopping, but the ugly thoughts were too much, overwhelming her. She collapsed, sobbing uncontrollably.

The body had been discovered at a disused cement works in Northfleet, Kent. Hannah had been dumped in a very overgrown area adjacent to a lake known as the Blue Lake. Land was being cleared for the Channel Tunnel rail link and the Ebbsfleet Railway Station development. A JCB digger had been clearing the heavy undergrowth to make way for this development when the driver had noticed what turned out to be Hannah's body. If it were not for his vigilance, the fact is that Hannah may never have been found. We'll spare you the gory details, but take it from us, what he saw was just horrible.

The Kent Police, headed by the senior investigating officer, Detective Superintendent Colin Murray, moved swiftly – much more swiftly than the Met Police had ever done. As soon as they found and identified Hannah, they came to Berni's home, talked to everyone Hannah knew, collected her belongings and searched her mobile-phone records.

More than that, they kept Berni in the loop. They talked things through with her and provided her with someone to speak to if she needed it. The one who Berni remembers the most was Detective Sergeant Colin Dutton.

DS Dutton wasn't just an outstanding police officer; he was a real person with a good heart who cared about what happened to Hannah and her family. He always had time for Berni and did more than he will ever know to help restore her faith in the police (as well as earning himself a place on the 'Our Heroes' section of our website).

By 23 March, just over a week later, Detective Superintendent Murray and his team had identified Robert Howard as their chief suspect and arrested him. Before you could say, 'Hannah Williams was not a runaway,' he'd been charged. Police had uncovered a video of Hannah in his home. Filmed by him, it showed nothing sinister but did prove that he knew Hannah.

During the trial, the jury were told how Howard had targeted Hannah. The court heard that Hannah was a teenager with learning difficulties and that Howard had exploited her vulnerability, grooming her for over a year until April 2001, when she was last seen at a market in Deptford. It is believed that he lured Hannah to her death; the exact details of how were never firmly established, as Howard denied killing Hannah.

The court heard powerful evidence linking Howard to Hannah's death. He had good knowledge of the area, and a blue tarpaulin used to cover her body was linked to him through his girlfriend's house in Kent. In a rare move, the prosecution were able to bring in 'similar-fact' evidence before the jury detailing Howard's past, which included the allegation that he had murdered Arlene Arkinson and raped a sixteen-year-old girl. One of Howard's previous victims, by now in her twenties, relived her ordeal before the court, and the jury also heard from Arlene's friends and sister about her disappearance.

If you're thinking that you've never heard of this kind of evidence being admitted in court before, well, that's because normally this kind of evidence is thought to be too prejudicial to put before a jury. On this occasion, though, the prosecution argued that it showed Hannah's death was similar to other cases linked to Howard, and they were right. One similarity was that Howard had tied a noose round the neck of the sixteen-year-old, similar to the way the rope had been found round Hannah's neck. There was also an allegation that Howard had indecently assaulted other young children (who had learning difficulties, too) at the same cement works where Hannah's body was found, and that he had done so in the months after he had dumped Hannah's body there. He was later charged for these offences, though it was decided that the charges would remain 'on file'.

In October 2003, after hearing most of this evidence, the jury filed back into the court after just three hours and found Howard guilty of Hannah's murder. Jury members sobbed as the full details of his other convictions, dating right back to the 1960s, were read out. He was sentenced to life.

While Howard was awaiting trial for Hannah's murder, he was arrested and charged for Arlene's murder, even though her body remained missing. The result of his trial for the murder of Hannah was kept out of the public eye in order that it shouldn't prejudice his trial for the murder of Arlene, which took place in June 2005 at Belfast Crown Court.

Unfortunately, no 'similar-fact' evidence was allowed to be brought in at this trial, nor was anything of Howard's bad character revealed during the proceedings. Thus – and it makes you want to cry for the poor family of Arlene – he was found not guilty.

Everything had gone in his favour. Detectives involved in the case believed that he was guilty, and presumably when the jury discovered Howard's history, they would have been convinced of his guilt, too.

However, in a bitter, ironic twist, he had escaped justice for the murder of Arlene. For Berni, it was heartbreaking. She doubted Howard would have been successfully convicted of murdering Hannah without the help of the evidence from the family of Arlene Arkinson in court, and she said as much to reporters at the time: 'I cannot understand why they did not use the evidence from Hannah's trial in the Northern Ireland case. The jury [in the Hannah murder trial] knew about some of the other things he had done and they knew he was evil – I do not know why it was done differently in Northern Ireland. When I heard he had been found not guilty, I could not believe it. How could they not see what an evil person he was? Why wasn't the evidence about what he had done to the other girls used? It was so similar. It has left me so angry.'

The question she also had was, why didn't the Met

Police act when Hannah went missing? After all, when her body was found, the Kent Police checked her phone records and spoke to her associates, an investigation that very quickly led them to Howard, though by then, of course, it was too late.

What if the Met Police had performed the same checks as the Kent Police did, only a year earlier, when Hannah first went missing? They might also have come up with Howard. We know that Howard liked to keep his victims around for as long as he could. Could the Met Police have saved Hannah from being murdered?

The answer is, we don't know for sure, but the Met knew they had got this case wrong from the start and continued to get it wrong even after Hannah was found. An internal investigation was launched into the three officers involved in the original missing-child report for Hannah and they were disciplined for their conduct. However, their names and the details of this internal investigation and the resulting disciplinary action have never been released. Berni only found out about the disciplinary hearing through the newspapers, as a local journalist had made a Freedom of Information Act application. Worse still, Berni discovered that the three officers were later exonerated in another secret hearing. Again, no warning or explanation was given to Berni or anyone else. That meant she never had the chance to put her side of the case forward.

News stories at the time spoke of a cover-up, and when we learned of all the shocking details about this case, it prompted us to step in and offer our support and advocacy to Berni. We laid the blame at the feet of the then head of the Met Police, Sir Ian Blair. After all, there is a guideline forcing police to investigate missing-child reports of children who have special needs or vulnerabilities; it just wasn't implemented.

Meanwhile, when Howard was given a life sentence for killing Hannah, his tariff was not yet set and it was decided that it would not be set until after the trial for Arlene's murder had concluded. Now that it had, the court was secretly reconvened and proceeded to set the tariff so that in essence Howard could be free by 2018. Nobody advised Berni of what had happened. They didn't even tell the Kent Police until months after, which meant that it would now be impossible for Berni (or the police) to appeal the tariff on the grounds that it was 'unduly lenient' because they could only do so within twenty-eight days. It was another devastating blow. On behalf of Berni, we're writing to the attorney general to see if anything can be done, but we don't hold out much hope.

When Berni found out about the tariff hearing, it brought the whole injustice of this case back to her. 'He can't come out,' she told me. 'He should never be freed. How could anyone even think of letting him out to do it again?'

She's angry at the system, and the police, and she has every right to be.

'I'll never know whether or not the Met Police missed a chance at saving my daughter's life,' she said, 'but I do know for sure that they made a horrible situation so much worse for me and my family, through some of our darkest hours, and although they did come back to apologise, it still leaves a lot of questions in my mind that I know will never be answered. I think we would have lost all faith in humanity if it had not been for my family and friends, the Kent Police, the Phoenix Chief Advocates and all those who have helped and supported our family since that terrible day.'

As her advocates, we were affected by this case on so many levels. For a start, our hearts went out to her and to Arlene's family, who are still hoping she will be found; we know better than most that finding Arlene will be the key to bringing her murderer to justice.

We couldn't believe that the judicial system hadn't been able to join the dots on Howard's history of violent sexual crimes. True, he'd been offending since the 1960s and archaic methods of sharing information meant judges may not have been aware of his past when sentencing him, but by 1993 there was simply no excuse. That's why there is a need for what we are calling Hannah's Law. It calls for a European-wide Sex Offenders Register with details open to police from across the Continent.

Meanwhile, with Berni and Hannah firmly at the front of our minds, we have made it our business to help train police officers in missing-children cases whenever we're asked, especially with family-liaison officers. Plus, of course, we continue to work with Sussex Police to campaign to bring in a nationwide (and European-wide) Child Rescue Alert. It wasn't available at the time for Hannah, but had it been, who knows, it may have helped.

19

We didn't have to wait long after posting a second message on our website to our mystery emailer before we received a reply. Once again, the contents were troubling to say the least. I now felt convinced that we were dealing with a genuine case of abuse. This was no hoax.

> Dear Shy and Sara we used to live near a bull ring now we live in the contryside I don't now where no family talks to us i cant rember them any way i cant tell at scool i don't go any more i never ever saw it happen this way its so sick if i tell you some things will you hurt me i think the baby belongs to em and i have to take drugs when it hapens they say. i can pretend to take them to get my head straigt and i will try to write a letter.

I immediately called Sara on Skype and she read the email as I waited.

'A bull ring?' said Sara, when she'd finished reading. 'They have bullrings in Spain. It would explain her broken English at least.'

'Yeah,' I replied, 'and she seems to have got the message about pretending to take the drugs. That's something at least. There's not much else we can do right now. I think we need to wait and see what she says in the letter.'

'God, I can't stand this – the waiting is doing my head in. Do you think the man hurting her is related?'

'I think so. Could be a step-relation, though.'

'I just wish I could reach into her life and make this better,' I said, shaking my head. 'I'm going to put a message up on the website tonight asking her to include a number for us to call. I just know that if I can talk to her, I can help her.'

Sara nodded.

'Keep your fingers crossed,' I continued, 'and let's hope the letter she's talking about writing gives us more.'

20

William Goad was a successful businessman with a fortune once estimated to be around £25 million. He began his career paying kids to assemble football rosettes to sell, then moved into markets and Cornish Market World, the biggest indoor market, then opening Ben's Playworld, one of the largest indoor play parks in the south-west, just next door. There, staff remember, he would happily sit for hours, watching the children play. What they couldn't know at the time, of course, was that he was a dangerous, predatory paedophile.

He's currently serving life in prison. When he was sentenced, a newspaper report noted that he was 'Britain's worst paedophile'; another that he was one of the country's most 'prolific' child abusers. It was strange to see the word 'prolific' used in that context, like the way busy authors or blossoming apple trees are prolific. With Goad, it wasn't books or fruit he bore in such abundance, it was pain.

His victims came from different backgrounds, all walks of life: good homes and bad. Some he gave jobs; some he entertained. Today, the lads remember that he used to take them out to restaurants and buy them toys and clothes. Goad's home overlooked a playing field and it was open house. At the end of the day, when most of the kids would go home to meals, homework and a clip round the ear for getting ink on their trousers, some of the lads used to go back to Goad's house. There were snacks and computer games. He had a pool table. He gave the boys money. He would be grooming them, before the hands on abuse started.

It could be in an office, on the floor of one of his warehouses, in his car or his van, in a hotel, anywhere. He'd use a number of methods to ensure the boys' silence. One was to involve them in the procurement of another child. That was it – now it was a threat he could use over them, to keep them quiet. Likewise, Goad would use the boys to introduce him to their friends or little brothers. One of the victims, Corby, was introduced into the circle by another lad, who was paid £50 for finding fresh meat. Corby was raped. At the end of the session, a £10 note was forced into his mouth and he was warned not to tell.

'You tell anyone and everyone's going to think you're gay,' sneered Goad. 'They'll call you a queer.'

Other boys were threatened. The usual way – threats against family and punishment beatings. Goad told one of them, Paul, that if he ever told anybody about what had been going on, he'd run Paul and his mother down.

There were other men, too. A boy called Chester was in the warehouse one night when Goad and a friend, Eddie Pratt, raped another boy. The boy was screaming and crying so they shoved a bag over his head – a red bag used for carrying money. One night, another lad, Ray, was forced to drink Scotch until he was sick. He was taken to a house where he was raped by at least five men. Passed around. Used.

Over the years, hundreds of lads came into Goad's orbit.
Over forty years of young boys. The court heard that he
once boasted of 'beating his own record' by sexually
abusing 142 boys in a year.

What was the result of all that abuse, do you think?
What was the effect on young boys of being force-fed
alcohol and drugs and sexually abused, often by a number
of men at the same time? Some went off the rails. Put it
this way: when Goad was finally convicted, in 2004, it
was on the evidence of some of the hundreds of boys
he'd abused. Records show that amongst all of the victims
there was only one mention of a petty theft, prior to them
meeting Goad. By the time they came to court, a few of
them had *hundreds* of offences on the books. Nobody is
saying that none of these lads would have ever gotten into
trouble their whole lives had it not been for William Goad,
but there had been *hundreds* of offences; all committed
after he started to abuse them. All these broken souls
hitting back at the world – a howl of frustration at a
society that had let them down. When you look at it like
that, you begin to understand the effect this crime has –
the *shattering* effect. Toxic ripples that touch us all.

Nobody understood that better than Judge William
Taylor, who sentenced William Goad. Looking at the public
gallery, he saw some of the same faces that had passed
through his courtroom with depressing regularity over the
years. 'It just brought it home with raw simplicity why
they were there,' he said, 'why they had been in the dock
and why they came back again and again.' The same
faces, year after year.

It had taken decades before those in authority began

to ask questions about William Goad, a long, tortuously slow path to his eventual imprisonment that began with one of his victims, Paul Wyatt.

In the late 1980s and early 1990s, Paul made statements that led to Goad's first conviction for indecent assault, for which Goad was put on probation. Paul also gave the police the names of other abusers and victims. (Paul has, incidentally, never stopped fighting on behalf of the victims, and is a true Phoenix.)

Meanwhile, a drugs counsellor, Phil Wilson (may he rest in peace), began asking questions. Why had so many of his young clients developed such bad drug habits in childhood? He persuaded some of them to speak out. One of those to do so was Ray Zolla, another true Phoenix. When he was an infant, Ray's mum and dad had been befriended by an older couple who promised they could give him a better start in life and offered to adopt him. His parents accepted. Unfortunately, the older couple beat him throughout his childhood. It was they who brought the pain into Ray's life. When he was eight, his adoptive parents left him at the mercy of Goad and others. They regularly raped Ray. Goad used to take his victims on stock-buying trips to Blackpool, Manchester and Birmingham, using his companions to lure locals into his van.

Once, when Ray was still a child, Goad forced the petrified boy to speak to another boy for him. 'Go and ask him if he wants to earn a bit of cash,' Goad told Ray, spotting a local lad. 'Get him to come to the van.'

Ray, too frightened to argue, did as he was told and the boy clambered into the van. Ray can't forgive himself for that. No amount of telling himself that he was just a frightened child can ever help. No counselling can chase away the guilt he feels. It destroyed him when he later found out that he wasn't the only one made to do it, that other kids were even forced to bring their younger brothers to Goad and his mates, and were given cash and booze in exchange.

Ray tried to tell the authorities about the abuse, but they wouldn't listen, so he tried to deal with the pain in other ways. For years he hid inside a ball of drugs and booze until he somehow managed to pull himself free of it. He met someone and she became pregnant. For a while there, things were OK. Ray looked at his baby and he saw a new life that was untouched by the horrors he had endured. He felt his baby's newness and purity and all the corny stuff you feel when you gaze upon a newborn: unconditional love, protection, nurturing and innocence.

This opened Ray up to the idea that the child he himself had once been still deserved protection and justice. Unfortunately, the adult Ray had little faith in the system. He had made a complaint against one of his abusers back when he was still a child, but the guy had been given probation, so Ray had taken the law into his own hands. He beat his abuser up and was convicted and jailed for GBH.

Despite all of that, Ray decided to give the police one last chance. In 1997, he gave another statement to the police about Goad. Days of interviews, page and pages of statements.

'Thanks, Ray,' they said. 'We'll be in touch.'

Nothing happened. Ray never heard from them.

Frustrated, isolated, angry and lost, he went to Portland Cliffs in Weymouth, jumped 139 feet in an attempt to kill himself but, thankfully, lived.

Shortly after that, on Christmas Day, another of the lads, Phillip, took a heroin overdose and died. He, too, had recently given a statement to the police about Goad. He was twenty-eight.

However, by this time, a police investigation called Operation Emotion was underway. Goad, who knew he was being investigated, had changed his name to David Scott and moved to Ivybridge in Devon. Then, once he realised his past wasn't going to go away, he got himself a fake passport and fled to Thailand.

Meanwhile, Phil Wilson, the counsellor, on the victims' behalf, lodged an official complaint about the lack of police action. Once again, it came to nothing. Instead, the case was passed on to another lone detective, who didn't obtain an extradition order. Goad remained in Thailand, and barring the odd statement here and there, the case stayed cold until 2003, when, thanks to a sharp-eyed bank employee, the police had news that Goad was back in the UK and using his credit card to travel.

Goad was on a train with his financial advisor and business associate when they swooped. He promptly complained of chest pains and was rushed to hospital – all of which served to delay the judicial process.

It was around this time that Detective Constable Shirley Thompson came on board and Operation Emotion II began, and it began in earnest. DC Thompson spoke to the boys, who were shocked to suddenly discover that the police had Goad in custody and now wanted their help to proceed against him. The boys knew he'd fled abroad, so had lost all hope of justice. As a result, whatever faith they may have had in the police or judicial system was long gone. DC Thompson didn't know it, but she had a job and a half ahead of her.

She had been brought in as a specialist child-protection officer, an expert in dealing with vulnerable witnesses. With the help of the boys and people like Phil Wilson, she managed to track down dozens of witnesses to corroborate the boys' statements, and she gained the confidence of more victims besides. In the end, she succeeding in getting seventeen victims prepared to take the stand.

Meanwhile, the doctors had put Goad back together again. He needed some kind of big-hitting heart operation before he was ready for his day in court.

At first, he pleaded not guilty. Even the judge tried to encourage his defence team to get him to 'see sense' in the face of such overwhelming evidence, and in the end Goad did indeed plead guilty. In his defence, Goad had claimed that he had been a victim of sexual abuse at school. They all try that defence, of course, because they know it might get them mitigation. Normally though it is just made-up propaganda trying to exploit the myth that victims of sexual abuse turn into abusers, and they know that the public believe the myth, however illogical that seems. Goad wouldn't help the police with any investigation into the allegations he made, though. Funny, that.

In court, Judge Taylor looked up at the public gallery,

where the victims sat, and as he later said, there sat the uncounted cost of Goad's crimes.

In November 2004, thanks to the efforts of all those involved in Goad's trial, the following day's papers were able to report that Britain's 'most prolific paedophile', a 'voracious, calculating, predatory and violent paedophile', of whom 'it is believed there has been no single defendant with more victims than this man', had been given life fourteen times over.

A dramatic case, for sure, full of twists and turns, heroes and villains, but there was something else about it that interested Sara and me – something about the wider issue of how the victims of child sex abuse are treated by society as a whole.

21

First, we suffer at the hands of paedophiles. As if that wasn't bad enough, we then fall foul of society's preconceptions about us. We call it anti-victim prejudice and discrimination. Most victims of child sexual abuse will experience it at some point in their lives, if not throughout their entire lives.

Now, the thing about victims is we come in every shape and size, every age, race, class, religion and profession. The majority of our kind – the 83 per cent, according to research – are what we call Phoenixes: victims who have risen from the ashes of a dark place to rescue their own lives, or who are trying to do just that, or who will, given the right support and encouragement.

Then there are the remaining 17 per cent. They're the ones who give us all a bad name. They use their victim status to behave like crap, and because of what they do, we all get tarred with the same brush. They don't represent the rest of us, but they do tend to get all the press.

There are also those who *pretend* to be victims for whatever reason – normally for sympathy or mitigation in some crime or another. They don't represent any of us either, but guess what? They get a lot of press, too. Indeed, whenever we hear of a high-profile crime, we can almost predict when we will hear that the alleged offender was a victim of child sexual abuse.

Thanks to that lot, some people think that all victims of sexual abuse are one of that 17 per cent, or all liars. Sara and I have worked with the real people behind these statistics, whose real lives have been victimised by paedophiles. We don't like to call them victims. In our world, we prefer to call them Phoenixes.

We accept that there is little we can do to stop the liars from exploiting the plight of others, but we must try to do something about the unjust bad press. We want to believe that our society can be fair and balanced, but when we hear how some of them think, it shakes our faith a little. We sometimes wonder if they know 83 per cent of our kind suffer because of what society thinks of the 17 per cent and the liars. Do they know about the prejudice?

It comes in many forms – from people believing the old myth that all victims turn into abusers, through to the fallacy that victims are broken beyond all help. You'd be astonished how many times we hear the following damaging blanket misconceptions about us: all victims are mentally ill, are likely to become addicts or criminals, only tell for revenge or money, probably asked for it, are likely to be unsuitable parents or could become abusers or abuser facilitators. You don't exactly give us much of a hopeful prognosis.

In some corners of our society, there are still those who believe that paedophilia is a contact-transmitted disease – the 'one was near you, so it's probably *on* you now' school of thought. We call it VPD – for anti-victim prejudice and discrimination. It means that from the moment you disclose that you have been the victim of a paedophile, you are at risk of being branded mentally ill, emotionally unstable or a bad candidate for parenthood. You could find yourself shunned and even blamed for the crimes that perverted adults committed against you.

On the one hand, society will accept that you have been harmed through no fault of your own, but on the other hand, it starves you of the help and support you need to recover. It's like people want you to suffer in silence and get over it without any help and with no mistakes, which means never turning to the mental-health services, social services, alcohol- or drug-addiction recovery services. If you do, it could all be held against you and your credibility at a time when you need it the most – like when you have found the courage to tell the authorities or the courts what happened to you.

We've heard some real horror stories about how simply being an abuse victim can be held against you. Astonishingly, this has been the case even in a court of law, where lawyers use the fact that a witness has been a victim of child sexual abuse in order to undermine them, especially if they've needed help for it, and even more *especially* if they've fallen off the straight and narrow because of it.

As a result, many police forces and Crown Prosecution Services refuse to put a victim in the witness stand if they have since lost their way or turned to crime. This kind of discrimination not only denies the victims justice, ostracises them and starves them of help, but it also serves to support the offender and facilitate their abuse of children.

Which brings us back to Goad.

The Goad case was highly complex, a bizarre collection of extremes. It showed the contrast between the limited knowledge and experience of the authorities in the early days and the outstanding above-and-beyond brilliance of the authorities today. On the one hand, it showed how useless record-keeping can be if nobody is able to connect the intelligence dots, and on the other, it showed how crucial people like counsellor Phil's record-keeping was when it came to identifying the victims and convicting the guilty. It proved what happens when agencies don't work well together and then made us proud when they did.

When Sara and I read the story, we looked at each other in amazement. We both knew something that nobody except the victims and maybe DC Thompson could have known. We knew there was something very special about this case.

'You know what these guys have done here, don't you, Sar?' I said.

'Oh, yes,' she said, grinning. 'I just can't believe they've pulled it off.'

What we were seeing was different to what the outside world saw. To the media, it was the end of the line for Britain's worst paedophile; to us, it was so much more. It marked the moment that everybody – the police, courts, press and public – stared right through the victims' criminal records and fixed their gaze upon the offender. For once, victim prejudice was absent.

'Do you think they realise it?' I said. 'Do you think they know that they've made history, set a precedent, changed things for all victims everywhere forever? This

DC Thompson must be some be kind of miracle-worker. I just hope she knows it.'

'Why don't you tell her? Give her a call.'

'I dunno. I don't want to come over like a sycophantic nutter.'

'Look, Shy, you have said it yourself – we're quick enough to have a go when they get it wrong, so we should be just as forthcoming with compliments when they get it right.'

'I know, I know. I'm just not quite sure what to say to her.'

'You'll find a way,' she said. 'You always do.'

So I did. I sent an email to DC Shirley Thompson.

I spent ages trying to think of what to say to her. It's not easy thanking a complete stranger you admire without coming across all stalky, but I finally found the words and sent an email. Before I knew it, I had her number and an invitation to call.

'Hello. Is that DC Thompson?'

'Yes,' she said, with immediate warmth.

'Hello, you,' I said. 'My name is Shy Keenan. I'm one of the Phoenix Chief Advocates and I am just calling to thank the boys, you and your team for the amazing mountain you have just moved on behalf of all victims of child sexual abuse everywhere.'

She seemed so pleased to hear from me, thanking me in an 'I was only doing my job' kind of way as I tried to explain the wider implications of what she'd done – what it meant for those in my field. I told her that we would be honouring both the police and the boys involved in this case by placing their names on the 'Our Heroes' section of our website.

She seemed touched, but I could tell there was something not quite right. She should have been as pleased as punch with what she'd achieved, she had after all just helped to secure all those convictions, but there was something in her voice that troubled me. I spend a lot of time talking to people on the phone and pride myself at being able to read their tone. She struck me as honest and kind, easy to talk to and warm, yet something seemed a little off. Still, we talked for at least an hour. I didn't know it then, but I was making a true friend for life.

Before we finished that first call, I found myself asking her straight out how she felt about getting Goad behind bars. She told me that she was pleased to see he was finally where he belonged, but that there was more to do – she didn't feel like she could rest until everything had been dealt with. That uneasy tone had entered her voice again.

I didn't push it, as I sensed she didn't want me to, but she asked if she could pass our contact details on to any of the victims who asked for them. I agreed. We said our goodbyes and I contacted Sara to tell her about the call.

'It was weird, Sar. It was like she should have been so pleased, but something was in the way.'

'Maybe it's just the copper in her. You know how they can sometimes be – sort of professionally distant.'

'No, Sar, that wasn't it. There is something else. I just can't put my finger on it.'

'Well, Shy, you're a private investigator – investigate.'

I grinned at Sara. I love it when she does that. It's like she knows me and knows that I won't rest until I've got to the bottom of something.

It didn't take me long to find out, because over the next few days I got to speak directly with many of the victims involved in the case.

22

'Hello,' I'd say. 'My name is Shy Keenan. I'm from Phoenix. We're victims' advocates. I'm here to help you find the answer to any questions you might have about the stuff that's happened to you. Our job is to let you know that if you need someone, there's someone here. If you have any questions about what your rights are as far as Goad's sentence or tariff is concerned, then we can help you with that, or if you need free help to make a claim for Criminal Injuries Compensation.'

It's normally an uphill battle to get any victims to accept that they deserve help or compensation. In truth, the guilt attached to victim compensation often proves too much and many don't make a claim. It's a terrible shame, as those who do claim and invest the award in their own recovery have always been among those who have survived well and thrived. That said, many of the boys we called were just pleased to hear from us. They seemed glad to have someone to talk to about the whole thing. For a good few, our reputation went ahead of us: 'Oh my God, you've called me!'

It was hard talking to all those damaged guys. I heard some heartbreaking stories. One victim, Ashley, spoke to me for hours. Now, Ash is the kind of guy you never mess with, just on looks alone. He's big, tall, with muscles on his tattooed muscles, shaven head, the works. He told me about how he'd avoided all of Shirley's letters and calls, assuming she was just another copper who wanted to rip open painful childhood wounds, only to dump him afterwards. He told me he had hated the police and wouldn't talk to them if his life had depended on it. It had taken him years to recover from the last time he had spoken to the police about Goad. He had managed to get off the drugs and wasn't prepared to put himself back in that place ever again, but something Shirley had said in one of her messages had changed his mind. She had sounded genuine and kind, so he'd agreed to give her an hour to see if he could help.

Even then, after four or five failed appointments, when they finally got together he took one look at her and thought, 'Yeah, great.'

He told me she was a five-foot-five, blonde-haired, blue-eyed stunner, well stacked with a nice—

'Hey,' I interrupted, laughing, 'steady on, you – she's married.'

He chuckled. 'I know,' he said, 'but she's the kind of copper any red-blooded male would want to be nicked by. But honestly, from when I first met her, I just knew she was someone I could talk to. Do you know what I mean?'

'Yeah, she's a diamond.'

He said he didn't mean for it to happen, but as he started to talk to her, the floodgates just opened. In the video-recorded interview, he started calmly enough, but then, he told me, he was suddenly taken over by an inner rage. The next thing he knew, he was screaming just an inch away from Shirley's face, spitting the words out like poison: 'That bastard raped me. He held me down and . . .'

Well, you can imagine.

Shirley didn't flinch; she just let him scream it out. The next thing, he was screaming direct into the camera, telling it word for word, blow by blow – how Goad and his friends had destroyed his mind, body and soul. He was bouncing off the walls like a raging bull, but Shirley stayed put until, just as suddenly, he collapsed in a heap on the floor at her feet and sobbed like the lost, frightened eight-year-old boy he used to be.

Shirley took his hand (she instinctively knew better than to try to hug him) as he cried out the pain. He held on to her hand like a drowning man trying to keep his head above the surface, and after he had let it all go, he sat back on the chair, emotionally exhausted, and calmly told Shirley everything he could remember about all of the abusers and victims in his childhood.

Ash told me, 'Something left me that day, Shy. Something that had been choking me my whole life.'

Shirley seemed to have this effect on all the boys I spoke to. She has a way about her, a non-judgemental approach that makes you want to talk to her. She is methodical and by the book as a police officer, but she also seems to care about the victims and it shows. What's more, the boys trusted her, and with good reason – she always kept it real, never made promises she couldn't keep and kept them informed every single step of the way. She believed them. She saw past the criminal records and the tattoos and she believed them.

And by God, it was worthwhile speaking to them.

They'd gone through what I had, so I had a real understanding of what they'd endured. (Well, up to a point.
I'm a girl. They're all boys. Something I can't understand
is how being abused in this way represents an attack on
your sexuality. How many times during those conversations did I hear 'I'm not gay'? It was shouted, whispered,
hissed. It's harder for men like that.)

From these guys I began to get a sense of their pain,
of the injustice they felt and the impact Shirley had had
on their lives. She'd pulled them out of the mental grave
they'd dug for themselves and got them to the point where
they were able to stand in the dock and speak out. Their
love for her was amazing. I've never known any police
officer produce that reaction in so many.

23

It took a few days before the boys began to connect with me and open up. Imagine you've got a nasty cut on your hand and a plaster over the top. Somebody comes along, causes you agony by ripping off the plaster and scab, then looks at the fresh wound, winces, sucks air through their teeth and says, 'Hmm. Nasty cut you've got there.'

So you grow another scab.

And it happens again.

That's what it was like for the guys – how it is for all victims of child sexual abuse. They've had the world and his wife tearing off that plaster for years and they're sick and tired of the hurt, so they either tell you to get lost or they simply withdraw. Can't blame them, can you?

If you want to look under that plaster, you have to work to gain their trust, but we had some things in common which helped to open the door. After about four days, we'd found out about some of the hidden aspects of the case, and I'd discovered what it was that had been bugging Shirley that first time we spoke.

Firstly, there was our old friend the tariff. Goad's sentence was 14 concurrent life sentences but his tariff was just six years and two months, meaning he could apply for parole after that period in jail, at which point he'd tell a hearing how he hadn't abused any more boys while behind bars, how sorry he was and how he had himself been abused as a child (omitting the fact that he had refused to help police investigate it). The tale of the dodgy ticker would no doubt get an airing, too.

I told the guys that they could appeal the tariff to the attorney general on the grounds that it was unduly lenient. I said that the judge had done his very best by them within what the law allowed and that I didn't hold out much hope for change, but that they should appeal it if they wanted to, if only to register their objections. They said they wanted to and we agreed to help them. Sara and I lodged the tariff appeal and waited for the response.

Then there were the other men. And this was why we think Shirley hadn't been popping champagne corks that day. She'd got Goad, but there were other abusers walking scot-free. She's a loyal, professional copper, which is why she hadn't mentioned it to me on the phone. The lads, of course, lost no time telling me about how throughout the case they'd been telling the authorities about other offenders and were frustrated as to why they had not been included in the case against Goad. To be honest, so were we.

Paul and others had told the authorities about Eddie Pratt, others had mentioned Peter Norsworthy, and other alleged offenders had been named in the statements made by some of the many victims, but none of these had been investigated or charged alongside Goad.

They told me that whenever they brought the subject up, Shirley was always keen and worked hard to try and make it happen, but the powers that be seemed unwilling to take any further action. Indeed, when the guys asked the authorities directly what they were going to do about any further victims disclosing against Goad after the trial, they were told that the police would set up a phone line that victims could call to outline the alleged crimes against them and be given a crime reference number. That was it, though. No further action was planned, and no further investigations were being sanctioned.

The boys asked me what to do about it. 'Come on,' they'd say. 'You're an advocate, so you tell me, what can I do?'

They had fire in their bellies. A Phoenix fire.

'You want these other guys brought to book, yeah?'

'Too bloody right.'

'Right,' I'd say, 'we'll have to see what we can do.'

Later, Sara said, 'Why are the "powers that be" so unwilling to pursue, Shy?'

'Well, I guess they would argue budget, resources, jurisdiction, but if you want my best guess, I reckon it's the spider's-web splatter effect.'

'Which is?'

'Well, the problem is that every time Shirley nails an offender, another five will come to light. Every time she identifies a victim out will come ten more. It can all become very expensive for a single police force to take on, especially if it involves chasing offenders across the whole country and maybe even the world. I remember Shirley telling me that she could spend the rest of her career just following this network and taking them out one by one.'

Even so, we needed to ask the question: why weren't the other alleged abusers named by these lads throughout the Goad investigation being criminally investigated?

Surely this all falls under the now much-respected similar-fact evidence laws, but when we looked into why this information wasn't viewed by the authorities as evidence for further potential criminal charges, it was hard to get a straight answer. It seemed mainly down to the fact that the powers that be had not sanctioned the use of the police computer investigation database known as Holmes. If Operation Emotion police officers had been allowed to use it, it would have triggered official action and helped to push the investigation on.

The authorities were unwilling to make more prosecutions, even based on the evidence the lads had provided, including all the names they'd given. This evidence was known to Shirley and she *was* willing to act, but was powerless to do so without orders from above. Her hands were essentially tied. From what we could tell, there was definitely reluctance on the part of the authorities to spend any more money on this case. It felt like a false economy, a failure to protect and a massive injustice.

24

Sara and I made some enquiries to the powers that be. Our enquiries were met with the equivalent of shrugged shoulders.

Meanwhile, we were running up against problems on the victim compensation front. The authorities won't pay out to someone who has a criminal record and, as I think we've mentioned, some of our guys had criminal records. It makes you want to bury your face in your hands and cry sometimes. This whole process simply hangs victims out to dry. Take Liam, for example – he can't get compensation because he has a criminal record. Who knows how Liam would spend his compensation. But there's one thing we do know: without it, the odds are firmly stacked against him. We as a society are leaving the likes of Liam to get on with it. In about five years' time, you'll find them in the dock or in the gutter with a needle in their arm trying to self-medicate against the pain. The cost of having to fix that – the cost to the state – is more than if it had just reached out a helping hand in the first place.

Unbelievably, we discovered that the victims couldn't even get compensation from Goad, the millionaire businessman. This was because when he had escaped abroad with a false passport, he had resigned from his business and made another man sole director. When he was caught and tried, the jury were told that money from the deal had been hidden, so there was nothing left with which to compensate victims. His assets were safe. Moreover, at that time victims of abuse had to sue within three years of turning eighteen, which meant most, if not all, of our lads were disqualified. Forty years of abuse, producing *hundreds* of victims, and yet Goad's assets were safe.

Since the case, we've been promoting what we call Shirley's Law. We think that the moment an alleged paedophile is charged all their assets should be frozen. We think that the law should be changed so that anybody found guilty of child sexual abuse, exploitation, abduction or murder should be made to pay for the cost of the trial and ordered to pay all victim-compensation costs at the point of sentencing.

So who was there to help? Nobody. And what would be the inevitable outcome of the system's failure to support these guys? Take your pick. One thing was for certain: it wouldn't be pretty.

We, along with others, continued to work hard to get the lads the help they needed. Sara and I talked about what was and wasn't out there for them. We talked about the victims' expectations and what really happened compared to what could be achieved. Up until then, we felt really sure that the local authorities would clearly see the need in this case and set up the right kind of help for the victims from Operation Emotion II. No matter how hard we tried, though, or who we turned to, nothing was forthcoming. It hit us one night, talking on the phone. It was late; our respective houses were silent. Around us settled this horrible, terrible realisation that there would be no cavalry for the victims involved in this case, no white knight, just more pain.

'Sara, I think it's just dawned on me that they're not going to help, are they?' I said, my voice breaking.

'I don't think they are, Shy, no.'

I think I felt the tears before I even knew I was crying. I tried to draw breath to speak, found I couldn't. My chest was too heavy. I was talking not just as Shy the advocate, but as Shy the woman. Shy the sane person in an insane world. Saying, 'How can we get this out to the world, Sara? How can we get the world to listen to them? How can we help them to tell the world what has been going so wrong and what help they need to make it right? All anybody seems to care about is vigilantes and beating up sex offenders, but none of that stuff actually helps *us*, the victims. It doesn't bloody help.'

What victims need is understanding and support – for society to tell them and show them that they believe in them, to only look down on them when they are helping them to get up. Victims need the chance to show people that there is so much more to them than someone else's crime.

'There is something we can do, Shy,' said Sara, after a long pause.

'Hit me with it.'

'Well, you know your friend at *Panorama* . . .?'

I love how her mind works.

25

Obviously, I had some contacts thanks to the *Newsnight* documentary. As I said at the start of this book, when that programme was made, it led to the arrest, trial and imprisonment of Stanley and his mates, so I had some idea of the kind of power wielded by the media.

I began to have conversations with a friend at *Panorama* about the case, about how the police seemed reluctant to follow it much further, even though there seemed to be evidence of some kind of ring or network.

A week after I had spoken to my friend, the documentary was given the green light. They don't mess around. It was time for us to take a step back and let them do their job: *Panorama* would need to speak to the boys, to Shirley, to other police officers, to Judge Taylor, to social services and child protection.

Sara and I remained in the background, still working with the lads, but otherwise staying out of things, keeping fingers and legs and everything else crossed that the filming would go well and that none of the offenders they hoped to highlight would attack the film crew.

We encouraged the lads to start a survivors' group, similar to what we'd done with Phoenix but one that stood alone, and they did: Operation Emotion. (Incidentally, the police use a computer that selects the name of their operations at random. There's absolutely no rhyme or reason to it, which is why an operation to convict a paedophile can end up with an inappropriate name like Operation Emotion. Phoenix? I was just lucky, really lucky, to have a name that totally summed up what we were all about. Phoenix. I mean, God only knows what I *might* have ended up with: Jam Sandwich Survivors doesn't have quite the same ring to it.)

It took them about a month to make the *Panorama* documentary. Then the night came when it was broad-cast. I watched it alone at home, but not alone: I had the boys on about three phones and Sara on Skype.

Ray, our strong Phoenix, was one of those on the phone, virtually shaking the line with nerves. God, he's had a tough time of it, but things were, gradually, beginning to look up for him.

Sitting waiting for *Panorama* to start, the unspoken fear was that somehow the programme would end up doing more harm than good. I knew the guys making it, remember, so I had every faith in them, but neither Sara nor I are stupid enough to believe that we can control the media; it dances to its own tune. The first thing to remember when you're dealing with the media is that you've got a tiger by the tail. As soon as you get compla-cent about the tiger – the minute you relax your guard and say, 'There's a good tiger' – is normally the moment it turns round and bites you.

Then, of course, there was the fact that the whole thing was being dragged up again. Even if the *Panorama* people had done a brilliant job – the story the boys wanted to tell – well, that story was still very painful for these lads.

They'd been put through the wringer already. Now they had to go through it all again.

Then it started, the familiar theme tune. Overtaken by the moment, Ray hung up to compose himself. Moments later, he rang back, calmer, and we all braced ourselves. Not much was said, because we wanted to watch the programme. The lads had called in so we could share the experience with them.

It quickly became clear that the documentary-makers had found the story they were looking for; if they'd been thwarted in any way, it didn't show on the screen. Ray was interviewed, as were some of the others. When he was shown being interviewed, I could hear him sobbing down the phone. I just whispered to him, 'I'm here, Ray. Do you want to turn off? We can turn off if you like.' He said no and we continued watching.

Next, Judge Taylor was on, speaking about how he'd seen the same boys coming through his court over the years. The senior investigating officer on the Goad case was put on the spot, as were social services. *Panorama* had gone one further, too. Rather than simply reporting the fact that others had not been charged for the offences, they'd travelled to France, found Eddie Pratt and put it to him that he'd been raping boys under thirteen.

'I'll bloody well sue you,' he screamed at them, sheer panic on his face.

Me, the boys and Sara sat in stunned silence until the programme was over. As the closing credits rolled, the tears came in earnest.

The *Panorama* team had touched on the compensation issue and spoken to a representative from the CICA, who had confirmed, unfortunately, what we already knew: that if a victim has a criminal record, they are unlikely to get compensation. 'If you're raped as an eight-year-old boy, is that a good mitigating circumstance?' asked the reporter, Betsan Powys. 'It certainly can be,' was the reply, though the representative wasn't able to comment on individual cases.

Goad was a rich man, though – this was what was so galling. Really, he should have been paying the lads compensation for so comprehensively wrecking their lives. Once again, *Panorama* had done us proud. They'd tracked down one of Goad's business associates, a man involved, they thought, in disposing of his assets. Though again it came to nothing, *Panorama* was still highlighting some of the issues we felt were really important.

All in all, it was a job well done. Sitting back after it had finished, chatting away nineteen to the dozen to Shirley, the lads and Sara, I felt a sense that things might actually start to happen. The guys, when they were interviewed, hadn't been shot in silhouette or with their faces obscured. It was just them – the way they looked and the way they spoke. Speaking personally, that is the way I think it should be, except in cases where it is crucial to protect the victim. After all, why should victims hide away in shame because a crime has been committed against them? None of the boys went down that route. They had all been very brave and I was so proud of them.

For Shirley, the *Panorama* programme meant a massive amount. Thanks to the TV exposure, she was given the opportunity to return to the case and go after these other guys – at last they were going to investigate the case properly. Operation Faber was set up, giving Shirley and her colleagues three months to collate evidence and put together a report for the CPS.

First, she went after Eddie Pratt, who killed himself. You won't find too many people shedding tears about that, but it's a shame he wasn't brought to justice before he died; I think we would all have liked to have seen him in court. Peter Norsworthy was given fifteen years, and others were investigated for perverting the course of justice. Pretty amazing results for just three months, though we all wish she could have had more time.

As you know, we very rarely meet the people we advocate for face to face. Most of what we do is conducted by phone, email or post. It's a rule we keep for very good reason. The people we work with have either been betrayed by someone they trusted or by a complete stranger. Understandably, allowing a new person physically into their lives at this point can sometimes be too difficult. Because they have been betrayed already, and because they have felt their lives to have been invaded by the authorities after disclosing the crimes, some victims are very reluctant to meet with strangers. They resist help because they don't want to invite anyone new into their lives at an already very difficult point. For this reason, we explain right from the off that they never have to worry about meeting us in person. This is especially important to highlight to them when the case involves their children. We won't need to meet with or even talk to their children direct, as we can simply work with the parent or guardian. This gives those we work with one less thing to worry about.

In this case, though, the boys I was working with said they wanted to meet with me face to face. I explained that we don't do that. Shortly afterwards, we found out that the attorney general had agreed that the tariff given to Goad was unduly lenient and he was taking it to the High Court. The lads didn't have to attend the appeal hearing, but they wanted to and had asked if Shirley and I would go with them. Because the boys had kept insisting that they still wanted to meet with me face to face, I got special one-off permission to go along and support them. They were meeting in a pub beforehand. As you know, I rarely go out and when I do, believe me, it's not pubs I visit. Quite frankly, I'd rather sweep a chimney. I don't drink and I don't like drunken people, and since I find that if you don't want to get bitten by a lion, it's best to avoid the lion's den, I tend never to set foot in a pub. But the boys were worth it, so I made my way into London.

26

'Hello. You must be Shirley,' I said.

'Hello, Shy,' she said.

It was the first time I'd properly laid eyes on her. She was sitting in a pub in Central London, around her a huge bunch of lads. Together they virtually had their own section of the pub, as most people gave them a wide berth. This wasn't your ordinary-looking bunch of lads. Many people would consider them a bit scary to look at, especially in a group. In truth, if I hadn't already known most of these wonderful souls, I'm not really sure I would approach them, either. Some of them were over six feet tall, inked, muscle-bound meat-eaters, who could, if they wanted to, scare crocodiles for a living. They weren't scary to me, though; they were just brave Phoenixes trying to rise from the ashes of dark, terrifying childhoods.

There was a small cheer as I walked into the pub and I stood for a second or so, taking them in. God, they all looked smart. They were all suited and booted, grinning from ear to ear, all eager to see if William Goad's tariff would be increased, if justice would at last stand by them. Yes, this was a very special occasion. It was worth getting up that chimney.

And guess what? They all burst into tears.

I'd seen Shirley on *Panorama*, of course, so it didn't

feel strange clapping eyes on her for the first time. In fact, we'd become so close it felt like seeing an old friend. We had a drink (soft for me), caught up, then marched across to the court.

We were there purely as observers. It's not us who decides if the appeal should be heard, it's the attorney general, so it doesn't just happen on a whim; we don't send off our appeal and have our day in court as a matter of course. We wouldn't have any influence on proceedings. It was the attorney general's show – his office was making the appeal in the hope of getting the tariff raised from six years to at least ten years.

It was turned down. That's all there is to say about that, really. We'd sat in the pub with hopes high and had them dashed. You win some, you lose some. You pick yourself up, dust yourself down and get back into the fight.

It wasn't a great day for justice, but in another way it was a great day, because I got to spend a lot of time with the boys and Shirley. I really bonded with Shirley and we became the best of friends. We've stayed friends, too. I see her more as a little sister than a fellow child protector and I love her to bits. We can talk for hours about life, the universe and everything, and we often do – into the wee small hours. We have a lot in common and both have a very straightforward approach to the crap that life can sometimes kick up. We have a similar inner strength, though recently Fate has really put Shirley's inner strength to the test, as over the past few years she has been fighting for her life after being diagnosed with one of the worst kind of cancers and, just as you would expect, she has fought hard.

Dear Fate, you suck. Please give Shirley a chance. She has helped to make such a positive difference in so many people's lives. She is truly one in a billion and this world needs her to stay here with us. Dear Cancer, we hate you. How could you be in the same room with the likes of Goad and Shirley and end up picking on Shirley? And Cancer, we all hope *you* lose.

27

Some time passed before we received the letter that the mystery Spanish girl had promised to send.

'A letter has just come in from our Spanish girl, Sar. I'll fax a copy through to you. She's going to try to give us a number. I think we've got to speak to her.'

I pressed send on the fax machine and it whirred into action.

Dear Shy and Sara i read your story on the interknit and i am filled with hope you so strong i did what you said Shy and my head is bits better now. things are bad here it started with me its only me and it will be the baby next i want to change it so that nothing happens again. i didnt want to say to much because im scared. they always try and make me come like a dirty animal and then say its my fault. i don't want to do it but i have never seen it hapen like this before. when it does some times hapen a bit like this every one says nothing bad hapend so i don't know the words to say to make you see. i told befor she never stoped it and they died. if i tell will you help me or will you hate me forver can you stop them from hurting the baby. i have gone nearly 4 days without the drugs and things are worst now i can rember every thing i don't know a number to give you

i will send it to you with a time thank you for helping
me.

'Well, Sar, what do you think?'

'I think we're close, but you're right, we need to talk
to her.'

'Something's not right about this letter, Sara. It's like
the answer is staring at me in the face, but I can't see it.
It's driving me crazy.'

'Well, there's nothing we can do until we talk to her
direct. All we can do is wait and see if she will send us
a number. Then you can use your "victim-whisperer"
powers to suss her out one way or the other. Let's see if
she will send us a number.'

28

It was a lazy Sunday morning and Sara was getting some well-earned time off, snoozing the morning away, when the phone rang. Still sleepy, she picked it up automatically and said hello.

'Hello,' came the well-spoken Scottish voice on the other end. 'Is that Sara?'

'Er, yes,' she replied, as she searched her memory for who the voice belonged to.

'Hello. It's John, John Reid.'

Sara suddenly sprang to life and sat up, now aware that she was talking to the home secretary, while lounging about in her bed.

She didn't tell him, obviously, but continued the conversation with an inner smile. Once finished, she made sure to tell me that she'd just been in bed chatting to the home secretary.

A nice bit of comic relief, especially considering the reason for his call.

He'd rung to explain that a judge, misunderstanding a Home Office memo, had mistakenly released a sex offender; that the media knew about it and were about to get in touch. He had just wanted a chance to explain what had happened before the you-know-what made contact with the air-conditioning.

He was right about the media: in no time at all, the phones were going, our inboxes were bulging, and people were working hard to make sure the same mistake wasn't made again.

This wasn't the first and certainly wouldn't be the last time we would come up against a misguided judiciary though, and we had to learn two things very quickly about the law. First, when it comes to the law, never assume anything; second, for every law there will always be a legal loophole.

For example, the law in this country says that there are two crimes for which you cannot be given a police caution: murder and rape. Well, we found out to our horror that this just isn't true. You can in fact admit to the rape of a three-year-old baby boy and be given a police final warning. That's what happened in the case of Ann and Lewis.

Lewis was once a chatty little boy. A Manchester United fan, Wayne Rooney was his hero. He dressed up in the gear and tried to copy Rooney's moves. Lewis lived with his mother, Ann, and his older brothers. He had a normal, carefree three-year-old's life.

Then something changed.

At first it was just a feeling Ann had, an instinct. She was troubled about Lewis; there was something different about him, something she couldn't put her finger on. Then he began to behave strangely. He became very clingy and acted oddly when he had to use the toilet. He was reluctant to play out in their back garden, which adjoined their neighbours' garden and was a safe, accessible space. Suddenly, Lewis no longer wanted to go there.

Initially, Ann put it down to a childhood phase, until

one Sunday when her world turned upside down and inside out. Lewis broke down and told her what her neighbour's teenage son had been doing to him. The abuse had been going on for months and months. It was emotional, physical and sexual abuse. On one terrifying occasion, Lewis said that the sexual attack had been so vicious that he had been able to feel the pain in his stomach. When it had finally stopped, he had smelled poo; it had been all over both him and his attacker.

Horrified, Ann suddenly realised why Lewis had become so upset about using the toilet, why he had grown so clingy and why he didn't want to play in the garden anymore. It was not a phase he was going through; it was abject fear. She began to reassess her son's behaviour in the light of what she now knew – how he'd gone from being so good at using the toilet, so proud of himself, to utterly petrified.

Now, he would take off all his clothes before he would sit on the toilet because he was terrified of getting poo on his clothes. He had to have the door open at all times or he would become distressed. He'd take hours to go and when he finally did, he refused to wipe himself, insisting his mother did it. He told her he hated the smell. He didn't want to touch it or see it.

It all suddenly made sense to Ann. He associated the sight and smell of the toilet with the pain of the rape. Just thinking of sitting on the toilet would bring back horrific memories of the attacks. Thinking about it, she now remembered him becoming disproportionately upset if he got chocolate or mud on his clothes – or even if he saw it on anyone's clothes.

He had – in just a few short months – gone from being a happy, talkative boy to a withdrawn and fearful child. And now she knew why.

On that terrible Sunday, something inside Ann died.

Fighting back the tears, she hugged her baby boy and told him how brave he was for telling her. She promised him that she would never let another living soul hurt him again; she told him that the police would stop his abuser and punish him. And she believed what she told him. Little did she know what was really about to happen.

The following day, Monday, the police sent a WPC to the house to take a statement. On Wednesday, an officer and a social worker turned up at the house to assess Lewis, to see whether he had the cognitive skills to be interviewed on camera. It's not unusual for the authorities to dismiss cases involving children under five, saying the process might prove too traumatic, or the child isn't capable of providing a testimony for whatever reason. It was then that things began to go wrong.

Ann didn't even know about the visit until nine o'clock that morning, nor was she told that Lewis was being assessed. Picture the scene. You have a concerned but fairly calm parent trying to keep it together for her frightened, clingy little boy, when two plain-clothed female strangers walk into the house.

Within moments, Lewis was led away to his bedroom by one of the women. He freaked out because she was a stranger to him and he was being led away at a time when he needed to feel close to his mother to feel safe. The two visitors attempting to control the situation did so by keeping Lewis and Ann apart, which made things even worse for Lewis.

Ann pleaded with the women to let her try and calm Lewis, but they refused. You have to assume they thought they knew what they were doing, that they felt they were acting in the best interests of Lewis, of Ann, of the case. But they weren't. Instead, they were pouring petrol on the flames. By the end of the brief visit, they were telling Ann that if she insisted on pursuing the allegations, she risked scarring her child for life. They told her that the court case would be too traumatic for someone so young.

Surely, Ann said, they could at least take a statement. No, was the reply, Lewis was not suitable for a video interview. The case would not go to court, she was told, and after forty soul-destroying minutes, the officer and social worker told Ann to keep a note of any further disclosures made by Lewis and left her to it.

On Thursday, the mother of the teenage neighbour called the police to say her son had confessed to sexually abusing Lewis, and by Friday the police had a statement to that effect.

Shortly afterwards, Ann sent in a full notebook of more distressing disclosures made by Lewis. Again she pleaded with the authorities to officially interview her son, but they still refused. Instead, they offered to send round a retired police officer in an old uniform, who would pretend to 'interview' Lewis to make him think he was talking to a real policeman. Ann knew it would have been a lie, though, and she wanted no part in it.

Meanwhile, the authorities involved were playing down the crimes. One report implied that a particular assault was little more than mutual oral sex. It defies belief, doesn't it? It was as if they were talking about consensual sex, rather than the horrendous long-term sexual abuse of a three-and-a-half-year-old child.

Out of the blue, the neighbour admitted to a further seven serious sexual offences against Lewis. Still the police were adamant that they had no plans to interview Lewis. Instead, they planned to give the neighbour a final warning and place him on the Sex Offenders Register for twelve months. Oh, yes, and they would ask him to undertake voluntary sex-offender counselling for six months.

Ann hit the roof. 'Why?' she wanted to know. Why was no appropriate action being taken against this offender?

He was just a young adult going through a phase, she was told. This sort of thing happens a lot; we don't, as a rule, convict or jail this type of offender. When she insisted, they implied that she was simply out for revenge. When she tried to warn other parents of the risk posed by this guy, she was told to lay off and respect the offender's human rights.

In desperation, she got in touch with us, sending us a letter that left us speechless with disbelief. And believe us, we don't get speechless easily.

I remember thinking, She must be mistaken. This can't be right. I'm no legal genius, but I do know a bit about the laws regarding sex offences against children and what she was telling us just didn't make any sense. The law is absolutely clear on this, with no room for misunderstanding or legal gymnastics: you can't be given a caution for child rape. Yet there it was, in black and white.

Here was a woman and her son who had been so let

down that she wrote at the end of her letter that she didn't even expect a response – just thanked us for opening it.

It was one of those cases that made us want to weep. We implore victims to tell. It's one of our mantras. Find a way to tell – the sooner, the better. Sadly, it's not a message that's getting through. At the moment, we're looking at an average of ten years plus before the victim finds the courage to tell.

Yet here we had Lewis, a brave little soul who told his mummy within twelve months of the abuse starting. You'd think – no, you'd hope and believe – that given such tremendous courage, the authorities would act immediately and do the right thing by this child, thus sending a clear message to all victims and offenders.

But no.

Once again we found ourselves having to fight the corner of yet another family targeted by a paedophile, then badly let down by the system. I know what it's like – I know how it feels to shout and for your cries to be ignored, for your pleas to fall on deaf ears.

'I'll talk to her,' I told Sara. 'You do research.'

'OK, but please let her know that I'm here for her and that we'll all work together to see what we can do.'

I gathered myself and dialled her number, mentally rehearsing what I was about to say, sure of just one thing: she'd be pleased to hear from someone. She'd be grateful that at last her voice was being heard. Well, I was wrong about that. Shock, hurt and mistrust ran through her like words through a stick of rock. It was as if her fight with the system had somehow altered her genetic make-up.

'System-weary', we call it. That was Ann. She'd lost any faith she'd once had, and she'd had it in spades: she was the kind of person who'd trust a policeman and take the doctor's advice without question. Now, though, she was angry. And like any tigress protecting her young, she was in fight mode. She ranted, she cried, she tried to tell me everything at the same time, she leaped from one thing to another, she screamed. Over and over again she insisted that she trusted no one.

It took some time to calm her down. I verbally had to slap her face to bring her back from the brink.

'Ann,' I shouted, talking over her, 'just listen, sweetheart. Stop talking and just listen.'

She fell silent.

'I can't promise you that we can fix all of this, but I will tell you this: Sara and I have heard your voice and we are here to see what we can do to help. You're not going mad – they just want you to think you are so that you'll go away and stop pointing out their failures. As for me, I'm going nowhere. They are wrong and you are right. I will stay by your side for as long as you need me, until we figure this out. Do you understand?'

Then after a long silence, during which I was sure she was about to hang up, she burst into tears. She sobbed, utterly defeated tears. I cried a silent tear myself, as I felt her let go of her fears and finally let me in.

'How?' she asked me. 'How could this have happened?'

29

In situations like this, the offender needs time alone with the victim to commit an offence, but not that much time. They can begin to exert an influence over the child quite quickly. They groom the child into being frightened not to say anything. They threaten the child with things like 'If you say anything, I'll kill your parents.' They will use violence against the child, keeping in mind that they know a parent won't assume the worst if they see a bruise or a mark on their child. Parents don't automatically think, 'It must be from being raped or beaten up.' You just don't think that. The thing about this crime is that it literally falls from the sky. It is the last thing you are expecting to happen to your family. This is why it knocks people sideways so badly: it comes from nowhere and most people simply don't have the facilities to cope with it. It's just there, suddenly, in their lives. A dark, slippery stain they can't shift.

Paedophiles use this to their advantage, of course. They know that it's the last thing parents expect. They know it's the last thing anyone expects. One of their greatest weapons is the public's ignorance of who they are and what they do.

I'll give you an example. Many years ago, I saw an episode of *Kilroy*. I don't know if you recall the format of the programme, but they would have a studio full of people discussing a particular topical subject. This one was about paedophiles. Obviously, there were a great many in the audience saying that we should shoot paedophiles, hang them, send them to an island, put tattoos on their foreheads, chop their privates off and so on.

The audience had been told that among them were some disguised paedophiles who would answer their questions. I have to say that Kilroy didn't try too hard in the props department, as one had a fake moustache and another was wearing a woman's wig. They might as well have been wearing sandwich boards with 'sex offender' spray-painted on them.

Kilroy was speaking to the audience and they were sharing their views on which method of capital punishment should be used. The audience was getting increasingly aerated. Then the camera panned to the wig guy. Guess what? He was smiling. There was this calm, beatific smile on his face. All around him the audience was foaming at the mouth. This guy should have been shaking like a pig in an abattoir, but no, he was actually smiling.

I couldn't understand why he wasn't frightened. I was thinking, 'There you are, you're the paedophile Joe in that crowd; they're all getting upset and angry at you; you should be frightened.' He should have been frightened, or at least nervous.

I didn't understand, and I wanted to. I'd been on the show before, so I knew people on the team. I contacted them and asked to be put in touch with the wig guy. It's not something we normally do, obviously, but it was one of those times when I just needed to know the answer to something. I was consumed by it.

'Why were you smiling?' I asked him. 'What was it you were smiling at?'

He told me the truth. He said, 'The thing is, while you lot are talking about cutting off our dicks or tattooing our foreheads or sticking us on another planet, while you're all spouting that crap, we know we're safe.'

'What do you mean?' I said, hardly able to believe what I was hearing.

He said, 'Well, as long as you're still too angry to know that what you need to do is change the law, we know we're all right. And do you know what?'

'No. What?'

'If they hadn't been angry and upset, I would have said something to make them angry and upset. I was smiling because I didn't have to. That stupid woman going on about chemical castration was doing all the work for me.'

It had never occurred to me before that paedophiles actually do things on purpose to make us angry, that they like us to be angry. They know that if we're angry, we're not thinking straight. It was another light-bulb moment for me. Suddenly, I understood the tactics these guys use. They use our anger and disbelief as weapons against us.

Over the years, incidents like that have helped me to understand what we're up against – helped me to understand both offender and victim. So, of course, I understood exactly where Ann was coming from. Moreover, I had been in this exact place myself, too afraid to believe that help was actually finally here.

Once Ann had calmed down, she began to explain what had happened, and after hours of talking, I understood how a straight path to justice had somehow mutated into an unspeakable injustice. She'd looked everywhere for help. Victim Support told her that she must feel sorry for the offender, that maybe he had been a victim of child sexual abuse himself. This was despite the fact that the offender had told the police that he had never been abused and that he got the idea after downloading adult porn from the Internet. The list of failures was as long as your arm, every single one of them completely unjustified.

After seeking advice about the fact that the offender was still living so close to them, Ann had been advised to keep Lewis indoors. In the end, she had been forced to sell her home, uproot her family and move from the area, losing everything she had worked so hard for.

We could see that if we didn't help this family, nobody would. If they didn't get help, they stood every chance of becoming another lost or broken social statistic. Sara and I put our heads together and tried to work out a plan to help this child and his family.

30

We began by trying to find a therapist. No joy there. We looked, too, but were advised that there was no help available for the victim or the family, though of course courses were available for the offender. There wasn't a therapist within a hundred miles of the family, and neither of us had a spare arm or leg to pay for private care. Still don't.

Next, we helped Ann put together a complaint, but the procedure turned out to be a joke. They lost files and denied having conversations. They sent a colleague of one of the officers named in the complaint to take a statement from Ann. This officer refused to let her word the complaint as she wanted it and ignored her letters asking for it to be amended. So, surprise, surprise, after the complaint was assessed by the police complaints and standards department, they found that the police had acted properly throughout.

Ann was devastated, but had now learned to expect nothing less.

They did, however, send a police officer round to Ann's house to apologise if she had been upset by the process and they promised to learn any lessons from this case that they could and gave Lewis a £100 Argos voucher for being so brave.

Meanwhile, I'd found out that just when Ann needed me the most, I might have to leave her and her family to it for a while. The problem, as always, was money. All the work we do for anyone is done online, by phone, email or post. I had spent hundreds of hours on the phone trying to help this family and had run up a monstrous phone bill that I just couldn't afford to pay.

I didn't have the heart to tell Ann, of course. It would be yet another failure for her and Lewis to endure. Instead I kept quiet and prayed for a miracle.

Things were becoming desperate for Lewis and his mum. Lewis still had not conquered his fear of the toilet. He didn't want to poo because he didn't want to feel it coming out of himself, he didn't want to see it, and he didn't want to smell it. Just thinking about sitting on the toilet would bring back horrific memories of the rapes. He would go into the bathroom and be in there for five hours at a time. He would take his clothes off completely in case the poo got on his clothes, until he was stripped completely naked. Then, careful to leave the door open, he'd sit on the toilet for hours and hours.

The poor little mite. When he eventually did go, he hated the sensation of it so much he would sob for his mum and his mum would have to come in and wipe him, then spend hours reassuring him there was nothing there anymore, that the poo was all gone. He wouldn't be able to attend school and mix with other kids. Unless something was done, he was going to end up an obsessive-compulsive basket-case.

I talked through with Sara how best to help Lewis. Having kind of been in his shoes, I had come up with a few ideas that I thought could work for a child his age.

'All we have to do is find a way to show him that he can do it. If we could just let him see for himself that he can go to the toilet, his mind will do the rest for him.'

'What are you thinking of?'

'Well, please don't think I'm crazy, but I've thought long and hard about this and I think that Lewis may respond well to blatant weapons of mass distraction.'

'Uh . . . go on . . .'

'He likes these Bionicles toys, right?'

'Right.'

'OK. My plan is we buy the entire range of Bionicles toys . . .'

And I explained the idea, which was to use the toys as incentives. We agreed it was a good plan and we ignored the elephant in the room, which was this: *we have to buy the entire range of Bionicles toys.*

Because it was easy enough to say it. Hey, let's buy the entire range of Bionicles toys. There. I just said it, and it was easy. But have you seen how much these things cost?

I had a plan, sure, but it was going to be expensive. Plus, there was another wrinkle: that phone bill. It was the size of the national debt.

I didn't want to worry Sara – things were heavy for her then – but BT had come down hard on me. I still owed them £800, so they'd reduced my phone services to incoming calls only. I was now days away from being disconnected altogether.

Meanwhile, we'd launched an unduly lenient sentence appeal in the case of baby rapists Tanya French and Alan

Webster, a couple who had photographed themselves raping a twelve-week-old baby.

It's something we do a lot – appeal unduly lenient sentences when we think judges have been too soft on offenders. We often get raised eyebrows when we tell people this: What? You can appeal against a sentence you think is too soft? Yes, you can. Even if you're not the victim? Yes again.

Every member of the public has the right to appeal a sentence or tariff given to any offender in a crown court within twenty-eight days. All you need do is email the attorney general. If you can respectfully convince the AG that the sentence or tariff was unduly lenient, then the AG will launch an appeal to try and rectify it in their own right. You don't have to go to court or be involved in any way if you don't want to; you don't even need to fill in forms; an email or letter is enough to start the process. Clearly this isn't something the Crown Prosecution Service shouts about – you won't see adverts for this service during X *Factor* – but it does exist: the power to do it is within everybody's grasp.

That is what we were doing with Webster and French. They'd been given light sentences for pleading guilty, despite being caught red-handed, and the light sentence came by way of – yes, you guessed correctly – the tariff.

What we learned the hard way about the judicial process is this: when a judge hands down a sentence, don't bother cheering and heading for the pub because that's not the end of it. There's the tariff to consider. The tariff attached to a sentence is often more reflective of the actual amount of time an offender will spend in jail – if they go to jail at all. An offender can be given a ten-year jail sentence with a four-year tariff. The likelihood is the offender will be out of jail in four years or less. The only factors that tend to affect the sentence tariff are things like the mitigating and aggravating circumstances in the case – like automatic time off for guilty pleas.

After that, you have to consider things like the offender's right to apply for parole halfway through the sentence. Then, if it's more than one sentence, are they concurrent, consecutive or suspended for three years? Only once you've considered all this do you have a rough idea of what the actual sentence could be.

We find this process one of the most confusing. It's almost like listening to an annoying sales person who just won't tell you the price, who blathers on and on about added this and discounted that. If you ask us, the system should be clearer. We think there should be a minimum sentence that will not be decreased by mitigating circumstances but could be *increased* by aggravating circumstances. For example, you see courts giving time off to offenders who have pleaded guilty, but they don't take into account whether or not the offender was caught red-handed. Why should they get let off for pleading guilty to a crime when they were caught in the act?

What we'd discovered was that victims are never told that they can appeal unduly lenient sentences or tariffs in their own right. In short, the process wasn't being made clear to those who needed to use it most. So we spoke to the then attorney general, Lord Goldsmith. We told him that victims felt tricked, that we knew of people who had wanted to appeal certain cases but had no idea the option was open to them until it was too late.

Broadly speaking, he agreed and pledged to do more to make the service more widely publicised. I went away from that meeting in good spirits and knowing that, as victims' advocates, we were going to make it our business to ensure that everyone knew about their right to appeal an unduly lenient sentence or tariff. The French and Webster unduly-lenient appeal was, in part, a success, as the AG managed to convince the High Court to increase Webster's sentence.

When I first went to talk with Lord Goldsmith, there was one person, maybe two, in his office who dealt with the appeals because they were so infrequent. Now there is a whole unduly-lenient appeals office, and these days public appeals vastly outnumber those made by the Crown Prosecution Service. It's not a battle we've won just yet, but we're getting there.

31

It was because of our campaign to raise the profile of unduly lenient sentence appeals that I was invited on LBC Radio one day, on James O'Brien's programme, a popular, straight-talking radio show that asks the public to call in and debate the day's news and issues.

As our talk drew to a close, James asked how he could help us and I told him about the phone situation – how I owed BT £800. I'm not sure what came over me. I hadn't even told Sara, yet here I was blurting it out on public radio.

It turned out to be a blessing though, because the first thing James did was offer to bail us out. 'Would you let me pay that?' he said.

'Oh my God,' I managed. 'Yes.'

Now this doesn't happen often, but I was totally lost for words. Suddenly I went from sounding like normal Shy to speaking in a strangulated yelp as I attempted to keep my emotions in check.

He had some money set aside to buy a pair of earrings for his wife, he later said, as a present because she'd just had a baby. Instead, he was going to use it to pay our bill. He was as good as his word, and he's a true Phoenix hero.

Not only that, but off-air, we got to talking about why my phone bill was so high and I told him about people like Lewis and his mum. Next thing I knew, he was telling his listeners that he wanted to help us with a very special cause and that he wanted his listeners to help too if they could. After that, the goodwill started pouring in. By which I mean we suddenly had enough money to put the Big Bionicles Plan into action. Toys "R" Us, here we come.

We bought the entire range of Bionicles, from little pocket-money things right up to the big fighting station. We put the whole lot in a huge box and sent it to Ann.

'Right,' I said, doing the whole *Supernanny* bit. 'What you need to do is show him the entire box full of Bionicles, so that he knows that there's a beginning and an end. He's got to be able to see what he can potentially have. Pick the smallest one, and when he next goes to the toilet, put it outside the door where he can see it. Simply say, "When you've finished, that toy is yours. This time or next." No other rules or pressure.'

She did it. The next time Lewis needed to use the loo, she placed the toy where he could see it and told him it was there for him when he'd finished. He was finished in five minutes.

Next time he went to the toilet, the same again, except this time on condition he finished a little more quickly. He got that one.

Next day, you keep your jumper on while you're doing it, the toy's yours. He got that one too. Each day he was asked to do a little more. Keep your trousers on while you're doing it and the toy's yours. Each time the toy outside the door would be a little bigger, a bit more snazzy.

We were with the family every step of the way. Then came the final day and it was time for the really big test.

Could he go in, keep his clothes on, do a poo, wipe his own bottom and flush it away, wash his hands and come out of the bathroom? And could he do it all with the door closed? Up until now, remember, he had to have the door open. He *had* to. But that wasn't going to be acceptable at school. No, he needed to be able to do the whole thing by himself. If he did it, he got the big fighting station.

He did. He was in and out of there like a bolt of lightning, and he got his big Bionicles toy.

Even more importantly, knowing full well there would be no more toys, the very next day he was in and out just as fast. In the end, it was a case of Lewis knowing that he was able to do it if he wanted to – it was just a question of him knowing that he could. It took over a week to get to that stage, but after that he was fine. His mum signed him up for school and before too long he was socialising with other kids, which was our main objective.

The next thing was, he didn't like to be touched, not by strangers. We needed to help him fight his fear of leaving his mum's side and go out to play in his safe garden. I knew from personal experience that you have to try and nip these things in the bud. You can't let them drag on or you could end up in a bad place for years. If you can beat it at four or five years old, it gives you a better chance for your future.

As I said earlier, before the assaults, he'd been mad keen about football, which is all about touching, about banging in, kicking the ball, nicking the ball, trying to get past the defence . . . In short, you can't play football if you're worried about being touched or about going out.

For this, I was going to have to bring in the big guns.

I would need his hero, Wayne Rooney, to help. Everything Wayne Rooney said was God's word as far as Lewis was concerned. If his mum wanted to persuade him to do something, for example, one sure-fire way was to invoke the almighty Rooney: 'I'll write to Wayne Rooney and tell him what a big boy you are,' she'd say.

So I decided to do exactly that: I'd write to Wayne for real and tell him about Lewis. I got in touch with Wayne Rooney's 'people' and (with special permission) I told them about this little fellow, fully expecting a generic 'Thank you for your letter, sorry but we can't help' response.

Within days a reply came back from Wayne Rooney, *the* Wayne Rooney: I'd love to help. Just tell me what you need.

Very politely and gently, we told him.

Within days a package turned up from Wayne Rooney. He'd sent a football, along with a handwritten letter and some other stuff. In it, he said that he'd heard that Lewis had been through a lot, but that he'd been a very, very brave boy. He said that he was enclosing a football for Lewis to use. He said that if Lewis wanted to be as good as him at football, then he needed to get out and practice.

Along with a specially designed award from us for bravery, we sent the parcel on to Ann, who told us that Lewis nearly exploded out of his skin when he saw what was inside the box. She sobbed on the phone. It was the first time in ages she had seen him so animated, so happy, and when he read the letter . . .

'Oh my God, Shy, he was practically screaming. Wayne Rooney thought he was brave. Wayne Rooney thought he was special. Wayne Rooney thought he could be as good as *he* was if he practiced. Well, that was it!'

He was dressed in his kit and out of the door kicking the ball around the back garden before you could say, 'Thank you, Wayne, for helping to rescue my son.'

Suddenly he had bigger, more important things to think about, like being as good as his football hero. He wanted to kick his ball and he wanted all his friends to see him doing it, because it was *Wayne Rooney's football*.

And, of course, because he was playing football with his friends, there was bodily contact and he was finally able to leave his mother's side. Before, he'd clung on to her leg – literally clung on to her leg – for comfort. Suddenly, he didn't need to.

Lewis will never get over his ordeal fully. He and his family will have to live with that for the rest of their lives, but at least we were able to do something to help him along the way.

If only we could do more.

Sara and I learned many lessons in this case. We learned that the law can be wrong, that the people who enforce it can be wrong and that the kindness of strangers can be a powerful force for good. We will be eternally grateful to Rooney for his help, but we both felt that the reason Lewis stood any chance at all of surviving what happened to him at the hands of his abuser and the system was because of his wonderful, loving mother. She let him cry when he wanted, laugh when he wanted and talk when he wanted. She was always there for him, she fought for him, and when he was safely out of earshot, she cried for him. She didn't accept that her son was now broken or beyond help. She always wanted the very best for him and worked hard to make sure he knew he wasn't going to be a victim for the rest of his life.

It was because of Lewis and other children like him that Sara and I started to campaign for what we call Lewis's Law, and still campaign for it to this day. As we see it, if a child has the courage to tell, then a video statement should be taken. All victims disclosing child sexual abuse should be video-recorded from the first disclosure, whether the police intend to proceed or not. This would ensure that the police assess the victim properly and it would also give all those involved a clear picture of what the victim is actually claiming. If it gets to court, these recorded interviews should be the first thing the jury sees before the victim gives their evidence in person.

32

The LBC Radio and Wayne Rooney incidents were wonderful occasions when we were touched to our toenails by the kindness of total strangers. We've been lucky enough to have a few more of them. Another involved Laurence Llewelyn-Bowen. Yes, him – the long-haired goth design guru off the TV. Him and his missus are total and utter diamonds.

He came to the aid of a little girl called Imogen, a beautiful ten-year-old who loved arts and crafts and was particularly keen on interior design. Her father was disabled and the home had been specially adapted to meet his needs; her mother was a full-time carer. They were a close, loving family. What they didn't realise was that they had a paedophile living next door.

The neighbour moved in on the family and gained their basic trust, until a sudden one-off attack.

Now there's good news, there's bad news, and there's really bad news.

The good news is that the next-door neighbour was convicted of the attack.

The bad news is that he wasn't jailed.

The really bad news is that he was allowed to continue living next door.

Imogen had coped well with what happened – as well

as could be expected, anyway. While her attacker was in jail pending his hearing, she'd been having some counselling and making good progress.

After the conviction, and after he permanently moved back in next door, Imogen became withdrawn and depressed. She had even stopped going to school. Her counsellors advised her that she needed to get back to what she loved – her arts and design – but she told them that she was too frightened to imagine things because every time she did, her thoughts led her back to that terrible day. It was then that her mother contacted us.

We spoke to the authorities and helped them to understand why the offender should be moved. This was easier said than done, as he owned the house. Still, thanks to their support, he was encouraged to sell up and move away. The whole thing took time though – time during which Imogen was going through hell. Her parents couldn't move so they let her stay at her aunt's home for a while, but this affected her schooling even more.

She needs some inspiration, something to kick-start her interests, I thought. I asked her mum if she had any ideas. She said Imogen had been asking to decorate her room on her own for years and that maybe now was the time to say yes. Unfortunately, they didn't have much in the way of a makeover fund.

'Who's Imogen's hero?' I asked her mum. (I wasn't thinking about what we'd done with Wayne Rooney. Cross my heart and hope to die.)

It turned out that Imogen loved Laurence Llewelyn-Bowen. So, with her mum's permission, we contacted him, told him of Imogen's plight and asked if he would help us. The Llewelyn-Bowens were amazingly kind and sent us a massive box of all things Laurence. We added a small makeover fund to the package and asked Imogen to redesign her room in any way she wanted. She was so thrilled that her idol had thought of her that she immediately began redecorating her room . . . and without even realising it, she was imagining again.

Once Imogen realised she could do it, there was no stopping her. She went back to school and won an award for 'Best Design Project'. We've seen her work and she is very good. Laurence has certainly inspired some serious competition, and we will never forget what he did to help this wonderful little girl.

33

So how does Imogen cope? How do Ann and Lewis cope? Berni? Pete Dawson? The Operation Emotion boys? Fiona, Tom and Libby? Sara and me?

'With difficulty' is the short, understated and slightly facetious answer. Paedophile crimes leave a terrible, terrible legacy in their wake. They harm and erode everything they touch and they seem to touch bloody well everything: eroding the judicial system, the medical profession, local authority services, you name it.

For the victim, though, it's a whole world of pain. It's a crime that keeps on hurting on many, many different levels for their entire life. What's more it affects not only the victim but their family, their neighbourhood and, in many cases, their whole community.

Short-term physical harm can range from surface injuries and bruising to genital infections, mutilation and severe scarring. Long-term physical issues can include things like sexually transmitted diseases, childhood pregnancies and miscarriages, spastic uterus, incontinence, spastic bladder and colon, hip dysplasia, very heavy and over-painful periods, adrenaline disorders, irritable bowel syndrome . . . again, you name it.

Meanwhile, the emotional harm is almost impossible to gauge, because each victim responds individually. What we can say for sure is that there is *always* harm. Many of our kind suffer with things like sleep disorders, post-traumatic stress and depressive symptoms, which can be set off by flashbacks or other sensory triggers like smells or sounds. Many of us go on to develop obsessive-compulsive disorders. Others will self-medicate by various means – prescription and illegal drugs and alcohol – to relieve the symptoms.

It's so strange. You can look at your life and think, OK, I'm coping pretty well with all of the things on my plate. Life is good and can only get better. Then, in a moment, and for what appears to be no reason at all, the same plate can suddenly look hopeless, frightening and completely overwhelming.

As a consequence, we do what we can to look after ourselves. For invasive thoughts or flashbacks, we find that distractions help: soothing meditation music and sounds, for example, or videos. Stick them on an iPod and play them in one ear while you go about your business.

Invasive thoughts are often worse at night. They can be so bad they interfere with sleep. You can buy pillows that play music. Put two different very quiet sounds on and try to concentrate on both at the same time. Before you know it, you'll be asleep.

Some of us suffer with night-motion sensitivity. This is when any movement while you are asleep, even acci-dental touching, can startle you awake and put you imme-diately on the defensive. Not much fun for partners, and certainly no fun for sufferers. We normally advise these couples to buy a big bed and put two separate single mattresses on it. This will make it more difficult to sense movement; if it's really bad, get big single beds and push them together.

Other recovery tips . . . Write a song and sing it. Write your childhood memoirs, then put them away. Play memory games and problem-solving brain puzzles. Play card games. Plant and grow three things you can eat. Learn how to emotionally debrief yourself at least once a month. For everything you say you don't like about yourself, name something that you do. If you can't think of anything to like, stop naming things full stop.

If you suffer with massive mood swings, ask your doctor to test your adrenal glands and see if there is any treatment that will help. Never make a life-changing decision within three days of a mood swing. If your relationship is struggling, don't leave it to flounder; get some counselling to help you both work things through. If you have sexual problems, seek help to fix them. The bottom line is to do something. If left untreated, these symptoms can very quickly become serious emotional disorders and/or addictions.

It's a similar story when it comes to the families of victims. Again, we're talking emotional health problems, as well as substance abuse. There's guilt, recrimination, shame.

For both victims and their families, there is a high instance of relationship breakdowns – mainly around the time of disclosure or discovery. There is also an unusually high rate of divorce for families of children murdered by paedophiles and in families of children abducted and still missing.

Most Phoenixes will tell you that these crimes are like

toxic cluster bombs going off in people's lives, eroding the fabric of society and damaging relationships. Obviously the more terrible the offence, the more harm done, but it is also true that the longer the abuse goes on for, the more harm is done. The more harm done, the more help will be needed to recover.

Part of the way we do this is to work together as a community. In our case, the Phoenix community.

34

Within Phoenix, we're fortunate enough to benefit from many people with individual experiences who together have an understanding of paedophiles. Ask the Phoenix community and they'll tell you that paedophiles use secrets, lies, fear and guilt to get what they want and get away with it. The best way to beat them is not to keep the secrets – expose the lies, overcome the fear and put the guilt back where it really belongs.

The fact is that nobody can completely prevent any crime, and paedophile crime is no different. But we're not defenceless. Whether paedophiles are known to us or not, there is a lot we can do to stop them.

Paedophiles attack in many ways. Two of those ways are a one-off attack or a prolonged attack. There are means of protecting yourself from both methods. A one-off attacker isn't going to spend any time trying to befriend or groom the victim or their family. This offence is more likely to be an opportunist grab-and-attack crime, committed by someone out looking for an unmonitored child. So when out, focus your child-protection energy on making those moments less predictable or frequent. For example, most paedophiles know that in public areas a good place to watch is the public toilets, so always escort your child to the toilet door and stay put till they're done.

As for more targeted victims, paedophiles don't much like communicative children from loving, invested families. These children are not immune, just less likely to be targeted. Parents can make their children less probable targets by clearly projecting their faith and confidence in their children. Don't be afraid to show the world that your children are loved and believed above and beyond any other living soul.

Empower your child with information and communication. Have the 'what's private talk'. The 'what's private talk' is a share-not-scare three-point conversation that we have developed to help families empower themselves and their children with the information they need to help protect themselves and each other.

Have this conversation with your child at least four times throughout their childhood in an age-appropriate way. Do this pretty much from the moment your child can communicate to some degree. This will generally coincide with when your child becomes toilet-trained, as you need your child to be both nappy-free and able to communicate for the talk to work.

It goes something like this: 'Sweetheart, now that you are out of nappies and taking care of your own personal hygiene, there is no reason why anybody but you should ever touch your private areas, except for a doctor and only then when Mummy or Daddy is with you. Your mouth, chest, front bottom and back bottom are your private areas and nobody, not Mummy, Daddy, your brother, sister, your nanny, grandpa, uncle, auntie, cousin, friend or teacher, is allowed to touch your private areas, nor are they allowed to ask you to touch theirs. If anyone ever asks you to do either, we want you to say no. Then come and find us and tell us and we will do whatever we can to make it better.

'If anyone ever asks you to keep a secret, you must say, "Sorry, but we don't keep secrets in our family, only surprises, like birthday parties and Christmas presents." Then come and tell us and we will do whatever we can to make it better. We love you and will believe you over anyone else in the world, and we will always be OK so long as we know.

'If anyone tries to lead you away from us, we want you to scream very loudly. Let's practice who can scream loudest. Scream, "Help! This is not my parent."' And then have a great time practicing.

As you can see, at no point in the 'what's private talk' has anyone mentioned the word 'paedophile'. There's no need to: this conversation is meant to empower the child with the knowledge they need to understand when someone else might be trying to cross the 'what's private' line, no matter who it is.

It is important to name all the relatives and adults so that the child understands where the line is and that this applies even to people they know or trust. This way, if anyone ever does cross the line, the child will know it. If the child has a good relationship with their parents, they will be more likely to tell sooner, hopefully before a crime is committed or before it can be committed again.

If the worst happens and your child does try to tell you something, how much they tell you will be down to you and how you respond. If you fall to bits sobbing, wailing and beating your chest, if you go flying out of the door with a frying pan, if you emotionally explode right in front of them, your child will shut down and shut up.

How the parent copes with this moment will determine how well everyone copes from there on in. We all do our very best for our children, but it's a fact that good parents aren't always measured by what they do when things are going well and everyone is succeeding – they're also measured by how they act when things have gone wrong.

35

When we talk to victims, we never talk about the sexual acts themselves. To our mind, there is never any reason to talk about them beyond the fact that sex crimes happened. We talk to victims about support, we talk about their rights, we talk about the investigation process and how they are coping, but we rarely talk about the acts themselves. Once we know the basic details, there's nothing more to say about them. Perhaps some people think we sit around talking about sex abuse all day, but we don't. We talk about support and assistance and if the systems in place are doing right by them and their needs. We can go for weeks without saying the word 'penis'. In fact, that was the first time I've used the word 'penis' this month. And that was the second.

We have other rules, too. If you threaten suicide, then we have to refer you to a professional. There are exceptions, but generally speaking, most times, that's what we have to do. Why? Well, the fact is, we're victims' advocates: we fight until we're raw to get your voice heard, to try to get you a better deal, to see justice done on your behalf, but we're not professional counsellors. Don't get me wrong – I've been there myself, so I'm hardly insensitive to the kind of despair that comes with suicidal thoughts. I've been on that ledge. We're just not qualified for this kind of work. If you are in a suicidal state you can't really put up much of a fight. You need to rescue *you* first. It is not for us to play counsellors at times like these, but we can try to find you a real counsellor to help you get back to fighting fit.

We also have rules about anger management. If a victim or a member of their family is threatening GBH on the offender, then we might refer you to a professional, too. Just to repeat, virtually everybody we speak to *wants* to kill the offender, but hardly any of them will try. Knowing the difference, that's the thing. We have to make a value judgement and differentiate between those who are working through a perfectly normal desire to see a certain justice carried out and those who have travelled so far down that road that they've already dug the shallow grave. Unfortunately, the system doesn't always understand the best way to respond to this very natural anger towards paedophiles and their crimes. How the system responds to the victim can often make the difference between their coping well with the trauma and them becoming completely bloody exasperated to the point where ordinary, otherwise law-abiding people are being pushed into taking revenge.

Sadly, at this very crucial time, the system often deals with victims in an insensitive and brutal way. This insensitivity is most apparent in the language used when answering victims' questions – the system continuously refers to the 'offender's human rights'. In fact, no matter what you the victim ask, the system doesn't have an answer for you, because it is essentially geared up to protect the offender's human rights. Why isn't the offender going to jail? Why are they out so soon? Where are they? Why are they allowed to live so close to their victims or potential victims? Why have they been allowed to change their identity? Why don't victims get the same help, support and legal representation as offenders do? Whatever a victim asks, the bottom line is that the system can't give them justice, help, support, protection or a sense of security . . . because of the offender's human rights.

Victims are essentially told that although offenders have acted in a completely inhumane way, they are entitled to more human rights than their victims. This is the way the law is, but we're not so sure that responding, 'Because of their human rights,' is the appropriate thing to say to a victim every time they ask a perfectly reasonable question about the judicial process.

Of course we need everyone to stay reasonable and deal with the issues at hand, but we also need to do all we can to *help* victims remain calm at a time when anyone's sense of justice or patience would be tested. As victims' advocates, Sara and I try to help people deal with that anger until they are in a calmer place. Given this help, the victims will, quite naturally, start to find their own way through.

We're aware that there are people out there who think it is fine to inflict violence on offenders. They can be a vocal minority. In our experience though, most people who are of the 'kill first, ask questions later' kind have a history of dealing with all things they don't like in life with brute violence. In reality, most people are not like this. Most people's initial reaction to crime is anger, but they soon calm down and stay on the right side of the law.

As far as we're concerned, seeking justice through violence is not justice at all. Going down that road is *never* right for the victim; no matter what the circumstances, there's always a different way to deal with things. Sure, we'll be happy to admit that it *feels* right, that it feels like the only action you can take, the only justice that's any kind of justice at all, but it's not. You turning yourself into a killer and spending the rest of your days in prison is not justice; it just isn't the answer.

We were once involved in a case with a twenty-six-year-old victim, a girl called Molly. Obviously Molly wasn't twenty-six at the time of the offence, but it's a fact that most disclosures about child sex abuse take place when the child is an adult. A common trigger is seeing their abuser with another child; it sets something off in them and the next minute they're pushing open the door at the police station. Another trigger is having a baby, and that was the case with Molly. She revealed that her stepfather had abused her when she was six or seven. The case was successfully investigated and the step-dad admitted the crime. Unfortunately, if an offence being tried today was committed in the 1970s, then the system gives a 1970s-style penalty, so the step-dad received a very lenient sentence. By the time he was actually convicted, he'd spent so much time remanded in custody that he only actually had to serve two months. Molly's immediate family were her grandmother and grandfather. The latter in particular was incandescent that the stepfather had only served a two-month sentence: granddad wanted to kill him.

Molly got in touch and begged us to speak to her granddad. She didn't care about the stepfather being released; it was her granddad she was worried about. She didn't want a good man doing time for a rapist, simple as that. Sara and I got together, and I then contacted the granddad, who was just as Molly had described him: angry. He was angry that the step-dad had spent so little time in jail. 'He won't have got better!' he kept shouting. 'He hasn't had time to get punished let alone get better.'

Granddad was as worked up as I've heard anyone. He was shouting and swearing. This was a guy who doesn't usually swear and who never swears in front of his wife. This was a man who had been turned inside out by this horrific turn in his family's life. He had been driven to the point of actual homicide by what he felt was the system's failure to deal with it adequately. He felt he had been left to pick up the pieces. And he was right. The step-dad had served a derisory sentence and yet he was now kicking back in front of *Neighbours*. Meanwhile, the family had to deal with the shockwaves – the disgust, the shame, the paranoia, the 'sheer fucking injustice' as granddad put it. All of this had built up inside him, built into a rage so pure and strong that he'd gone beyond rational thought.

He had an answer for everything; every single argument I put to him was batted away. It didn't matter if he went to jail, he told me, he was nearing the end of his life anyway. That road I was talking about? He was a long way down it. His blank resignation was scary. I was used to encountering rage, but this man had managed to take care of his affairs; he'd reconciled himself to spending the rest of his days in prison. He was angry but calm.

At one point in our conversation, he left me speechless when he said, 'Molly's case is just a drop in the paedophile ocean of crap, and my grandchild is not going to be just another piece of paedophile crap.'

What could I say?

By the end of the four-hour conversation, I was nearly ready to admit defeat. Nothing I said was getting through to him.

Suddenly, he started talking about how wonderful he thought Sara and I were, how much courage it must have taken to be us and how the world needed people like us for people like his grandchild.

Without even thinking about it, I just as suddenly piped up, 'OK, you got me. Let's go do it. I'll get his hair and you do his eyes.'

He giggled.

'No, really,' I continued. 'Sara and I could do so much more to help everyone from a jail cell. We'd be the "Jail-Bird Advocates". Just think of all the media and the trust and respect we'd earn.'

He started to laugh.

At last, I'd found a way to go past his anger and talk to him.

I stayed with it and told him I wondered if they would let Sara and I get our mugshots taken together so we could use them for our new publicity shots.

Somehow, it seemed that talking about Sara and I responding the same way that he wanted to was getting through to him. He clearly saw it as wrong and started to see that it might be wrong for him to do it, too. His anger started to thaw a little.

I added, 'I have never in all my life talked to someone who has an answer for everything. I think you've found the solution, I really do.'

Now he was properly laughing.

Talking him down from the brink by telling him not to turn himself into another victim of his grandchild's abuser, another crime statistic, hadn't worked. In the end, it was his love for his grandchild that saved him. Ultimately, he came to see that the best place for him was right next to his grandchild, doing his part to help her recover. After that? Well, more phone calls, more conversations. It's not like a few long chats and all your problems are solved. There are no solutions in our world, just a chance at a better outcome. In this case, we were lucky that we were able to reach the granddad and talk him down before things went too far, but we both knew we needed something more far-reaching to really tackle the problems that victims and their families were facing. For now, we were just doing the best we could with what we had.

When we try to help someone step away from the brink of acting on extreme emotions, we call it 'talkdown'. What we did with Molly's granddad is just one example. There are many more. There is even a sex-offender talkdown. Over my years as an advocate, I have studied and learned at the feet of some of the world's leading sex-offender experts and have been lucky enough to learn talkdown techniques from them.

To give you an example of how sex-offender talkdown works, let's say an offender phones and says, 'I'm out of my flat. It's four p.m. and I'm near the park. I've started thinking I want to offend.'

They're telling you they want to find and sexually assault a child. What do you do?

One of the talkdown techniques is to ask, 'Where's your mum at the moment?'

'She's at home,' they might reply.

By asking that, you get them to picture their mother. A turn-off? For sure, but it grounds the offender.

A similar technique is to ask, 'Where's your probation officer?'

This reminds the offender of the consequences.

Then you might start to talk about a court appearance, or ask, 'Do you remember having to tell your wife what you had done? Do you remember her face? Who else was in the room with you? Do you remember how you felt?'

Putting it bluntly, you need to reduce that guy's erection, and you do it by reminding him of things most likely to do that: consequences and reactions.

During my time under the tutelage of those sex-offender experts, I sat in many rooms with offenders. Once, I sat with a man who had raped and murdered an infant. He didn't *look* or *sound* like a sex offender to me. (That was a learning experience. In a perfect world, all sex offenders would look and sound like Stanley, but they don't.) For my part, I learned that it's soul-destroying talking to such liars all the time – people who have built so many lies around themselves are hard work. It was emotionally exhausting deconstructing all the lies they told, because the truth of the matter is that if people genuinely want to stop offending, all they have to do is walk into a police station and hand themselves in. If they can't do that, they can try speaking to the people at Stop It Now or the Lucy

Faithfull Foundation. If you ask us, there are plenty of people looking out for the offenders. Our job is to look after the interests of the victims and their families, and to try, if possible, to prevent this kind of thing happening in the future. We came to the conclusion that we didn't want to be Phoenix *Survivors* anymore. We wanted to be more than survivors. We wanted to start winning for a change.

As it turned out, that was to be the most difficult challenge we'd face.

36

'Sara, pick up quick. Our Spanish girl sent us a number and time. I'm calling back in half an hour.'

'OK. What do we do, Shy?'

'We talk her into the police station.'

'I can't see her going for it – she sounds so scared.'

'I know, but I'm going to try.'

'Right. What do you need me to do?' asked Sara.

'Well, as I talk to her, I will feed information back to you. See if you can confirm what I'm telling you as we roll. If you need more, Skype me. Are you ready?' I asked.

'Yes,' she answered. 'Let's go.'

I dialled the number and the phone was picked up almost immediately by what was clearly a male. I hesitated for a moment, worried that the girl might have been caught and all was lost, but I could tell in an instant that I was talking to the same person who had been writing to us all along.

He is a boy, Sar, I silently typed. *He's nineteen years old and it's his biological mum that has been sexually abusing him. He still sounds a little out of it, but he's fighting the drugs now. Oh, yes, and he lives near the Bullring Shopping Centre in Birmingham, England.*

We talked for a few hours. He told me his name was Carl and he explained what had been happening to him.

It was clear he wanted things to stop but just needed someone else to lean on while he took that scary step. After promising him we would be there every step of the way, he put down the phone and went straight to the police.

It turned out that Carl's mother was a crack-addicted single parent who had been sexually abusing him since he was an infant. She had been feeding Carl crack since he could remember and certainly during any sexual abuse. Every time he orgasmed, she called him dirty names and blamed him for what had happened. She had a new boyfriend, with whom she had had a child, the baby boy Carl spoke of. She never had a boyfriend for longer than a few months and all of them were also addicted.

While still young, Carl told one of these boyfriends some of what was happening. The boyfriend told the mother what Carl had said and disappeared. Carl's mother told him she had killed this man and he believed her.

Years later, after his half-brother was born, Carl started to worry about the baby and spoke to his mother. She took it for lover's jealousy and threatened to kill him and the baby, like she had killed the boyfriend, if he ever brought the subject up again.

Unbeknown to Carl, the boyfriend was in fact very much alive and still on drugs. He had long forgotten his relationship with Carl's mum, let alone what Carl had told him.

After he'd spoken to me, Carl told the police everything and his mother confessed. As far as the experts could tell, aside from having traces of crack on his feeding bottle, there was no evidence that showed the baby had been sexually abused.

Carl was coping well, getting over the drugs and learning to live independently from his lifelong abuser. As the case unfolded, however, there was still one more horrifying shock for Carl: the baby wasn't his brother, it was his son. Carl was devastated, but at least now he understood why he had instinctively fought so hard to protect the little mite.

In the end, his mother was jailed and his son went to live with a wonderful foster family, who include him as much as they can in his son's life. Carl completely disowned his mother and now lives with his girlfriend and their three dogs. Carl has been drug-free for years now and is studying hard to qualify in his chosen field of pathology.

It just goes to show what a little bit of Phoenix fire can achieve, but somehow both Sara and I knew that helping individuals wasn't going to be enough: we needed to find a way to reach more people, to help those whom the system had let down.

Part Three

The Retreat

37

Talking personally, save for a few good people along the way, I can't deny that as a child (and even as an adult) my own personal experiences at the hands of the authorities in general were inexplicably bloody awful. From the very first time I tried to tell them what was happening to the very last time I asked for help, it was a mind-blistering journey of scary life lessons into why us orphaned crack chaff don't tend to thrive. When I say 'orphaned', I mean it literally, but I also mean a child in whom nobody invests. It's a lonely, hard way to live and learn, but it's just how it is for some children. When I say 'crack chaff', as much as I hate this phrase, it really is how authority care can sometimes make you feel.

Every legal, medical and educational child-protection agency or authority has a system, and every system has its cracks. As an orphaned and powerless child in the care of these systems, you may sometimes be unlucky enough to fall through a few of those cracks, while others may find themselves trapped in the 'system crack cycle', being pushed from one agency to another through the cracks.

For me as a child, it seemed that if there was a failure or problem in any of the various authority systems, I would find it or it would bloody well find me. With no one to watch over me, a small army of abusive adults had a field day all over my childhood, causing me untold harm. In the end, I was made to feel like a piece of dirt that deserved everything I got and should learn to expect no better. For a good while they had me there.

Back in the bad old days, it seemed impossible to break this cycle of abuse and reach any part of the system that actually worked. When I finally did make it, it was like entering another world, a world in which you were made to feel like you mattered. It was a wonderful feeling at first, until survivor's guilt kicked in. The more the system worked, the better things became. The better things became, the clearer I could see just how bad it had once been for me and how bad it must be now for all those still trapped in the cracks and being failed and abused.

As a child, I didn't think it was fair and wished I could do something about it. As an adult, I knew it wasn't fair and I was bloody well determined to do something about it. This is one of the major reasons why I became an advocate – so that I could do whatever I could. The reason behind why I became a victims' advocate was defined for me after my own experiences as an adult victim of child sexual abuse, going through the whole process of trying to tell people what had happened to me and the subsequent judicial process back in 2000. It was to be another light-bulb moment.

I remember standing in the witness box at court giving my evidence. Despite all the love and support I had from my own family, despite all those good people doing their part for justice, I hadn't felt so isolated and unprotected since my childhood. I felt naked, dirty and very small.

It had long been made clear to me that this was the

Crown Prosecution Service's case and that I was apparently one valued piece of evidence in the public's fight against sex crime. On the day, the prosecutor's job was to secure the best possible evidence from me on behalf of the Crown. Nevertheless, once the finely tuned legal defence played three rounds of witness punchbag with me, I couldn't help but notice that despite my alleged value, of all the people in the room on that day I was the only one who didn't have an advocate or a solicitor to protect me. I wished I too had someone to protect me. I felt that the defendants' lawyers were attempting to mislead the courts about me and exploiting the fact that I didn't have their knowledge and couldn't have a solicitor, an expert or a character witness.

As the thought flashed through my mind, I started shaking. Then I started getting flashbacks of moments throughout this whole horrible journey, other times when I had wished there had been someone there not only to protect me but help me. I had wished this in particular after I'd spent hours dragging up dark, painful memories from a terrifying childhood for the police to copy into my official statement. The Operation Phoenix police officers were brilliant with me throughout this process, but they were police officers, not the counsellors I needed to help me recover from telling the police. What is more, and I understand that it was necessarily so, the police had turned most of the people I would have normally talked to into witnesses, so I wasn't able to discuss the details of the case with them until after it was all over. It was a very lonely time.

Remember, it's not so much that the system refuses to

allow you to get counselling during the judicial process – even if I'd had the wherewithal to somehow insist upon or organise counselling, I'd have been compromising the court case. It's just the way things work.

Standing there in the witness box, feeling like dirty system chaff again, the light-bulb moment happened and I knew then that when this was all over, I would try to find a way to make things better. Right then, I had to defend myself, and I'm so glad I did. By the time I had stepped down from the witness box, I was a changed person. Standing up for myself had changed me.

In the years since, Sara and I have talked for hours about this system, about how victims aren't entitled to their own solicitor or to proper non-prejudicial counselling during the trial. It seems a bizarre prejudice against them. Why don't victims of crime get more help and legal protection?

I said, 'Maybe it is just all about money. Can you imagine how much a solicitor for every single victim of crime would cost?'

'It's not just the cost,' said Sara. 'The involved agencies tend to view a victim's legal representatives as potentially prejudicial, so in between these two main concerns, the victim's rights get lost. It's about finding the right balance. To find that balance, you need to have a good idea of the real costs involved in both kinds of cases, looking at what happens when victims are helped and when they are not. How much does it cost to pick up the pieces? What is the price to society? Is it as much as providing counselling and advocacy for the family? As much as giving them a solicitor so that their interests can be represented in court?'

Take thirteen-year-old Jo, for example, another victim of child sexual abuse. His abuser was given two years' probation for sexually abusing him for three years. Jo was not given proper help or support, so he turned to drugs and alcohol. Not long after that, he turned to crime to feed his habit. Not long after that, he was jailed for stealing to feed his habit. Not long after that, he was using the drug and alcohol rehabilitation services in an attempt to stop his habit. They dealt with his addiction but not, crucially, the cause, which meant he was soon back in jail for stealing to feed his habit. Meanwhile, his abuser went on to abuse two other young boys, who began receiving mental-health treatment from the NHS – only it wasn't the right sort of treatment. Not long after that, one of those boys was using the drug rehabilitation services to help him with his addiction to prescription drugs . . .

The lessons here are obvious. If the courts had properly punished and treated the offender, he wouldn't have been free to abuse again. If the system had helped Jo after he disclosed, then he would not have needed to self-medicate. The real costs are spread among the various services and over many years, so no one single figure can ever be identified. Make no mistake though, the bill still has to be paid.

We see that victims are discriminated against across the board and it is never more apparent to us than within the medical profession. Victims of child sexual abuse have suffered at their hands for years, but the system has always demanded that they or their parents pay their National Health Service contributions. Can you imagine turning up at A&E with a broken leg and being told that they have no specific treatment for your injury, but they can give you a prejudicial note on your permanent files and addictive drugs to help you ignore the pain, and you can ring a voluntary group who can only afford to speak to you for an hour a month by appointment?

The vast majority of victims are not mentally ill. They are emotionally harmed and they need proper emotional health services, designed specifically for their recovery. Sara and I have had hours of debate devising magic wand, pie-in-the-sky wish lists of what we would put in place to help if we had the power. We've even checked how much all that would really cost, which is when we fully realised that big change will cost big money. But it would be big money very well spent.

We're not stupid – we know everything boils down to money, but in this case the less we pay now to help, the more we pay later. If we pay a little more now, we'll cut our future bill in half.

Sara and I were just two ordinary women doing our best to keep our fingers in this problematic dam. We'd used up all our twenty fingers and still the problems were leaking through thick and fast. We clearly needed a better dam. We planned to propose something – something big.

We called it the RARE Phoenix Retreat. The idea was this: we would set up a centre, a place that would act as a base for a team of counsellors, advocates and solicitors whose sole responsibility would be to look out for the victims of child sexual abuse and their families, as well as acting as a retreat with cottages for victims. This was to be our dam. The RARE team (the Retreat Advocacy and Research Centre of Excellence team) would be on hand not only to deal with individual cases, advocating for victims, standing up for them in court, making sure they were kept informed by the authorities and treated with the kind of respect that a victim of serious, life-shattering crimes deserves, but also with a remit to push for real, profound change. So when not parachuting in to aid on a case-by-case basis, our guys would be pressing the law for reform. They'd be canvassing MPs, talking to the law lords, campaigning, as well as developing templates of victim care to teach to all local authorities.

And Sara and me? We'd have the odd day off. Spend more time with the family, go fishing, write books and songs.

To get our retreat up and running, we'd need £3 million. But here's the thing – it had to be (at least partly) government-funded; we had to get the government on our side. Yes, we could have tried to set up a RARE Retreat independently, but doing that would have meant surrendering a huge part of its effectiveness. What we needed was an organisation with teeth that worked alongside all the existing government agencies. In order for those cogs to mesh efficiently, the RARE team needed to be a government-supported agency, too. For example, if you're a victim of sexual abuse and you disclose, you would immediately have an advocate appointed to you. But introducing this would mean making an expensive policy change. Independent bodies don't wield that kind of power. You need to be on the inside, so that you can get local councils and the police to abide by those templates of care.

So in a case like Sara's, say, in which the police are desperately looking for a private, comfortable place to take the family where they can talk to them, keep them informed, protect them from the glare of the media, they could scoop up the entire family, bring them to the retreat and put them in the cottages. No one would bother them. Help would be on hand if they wanted it: counsellors, psychologists, solicitors, advocates, trained people they need to help them recover their lives. In liaison with the police, the retreat would be available for them when they needed it.

The plan was to present the government with this idea, get them to make the RARE Retreat part of the process. We got our chance and told them why they needed to be involved. We had been encouraged to believe that the government might give us the land and buildings we needed, while we would have to find the operational costs elsewhere. It was a good start.

OK, so it was going to be tough – very tough. Our Phoenix caseload was already way, way too big for two people. We were, as usual, struggling financially, but we're Amazonian women and we're made out of girders, so if we wanted to do something about the dam, then we would. We set out on the Herculean task of planning our retreat.

38

Meanwhile, the cases continued to build up. We dealt with a heartbreaking situation involving the father of a baby boy, Charles, who was abused by his stepmother's secret lover.

The stepmother claimed that to avoid her affair coming out, she gave her step-son's abuser a fake alibi for the time when Charles had made an allegation of abuse. She said it couldn't be true because the accused never had lone access to Charles; she claimed that her husband might have made up the accusation for revenge because he suspected her of cheating. There's no way she would ever let anything happen to Charles, she said; in fact, to prove how much she loved him, she had applied for visitation rights.

For a while, it looked as though her smokescreen might save her. That was until we got some anonymous information that helped the authorities find her missing laptop computer. On the computer were films showing Charles and her perverted boyfriend . . . and her.

Paedophiles like nothing better than films and photographs to record their crimes, of course – a feature of the crime that often makes it into the public domain. This is one of the areas where we find ourselves working hard to change public preconceptions about the issues involving child abuse and child protection. You'll have heard the expressions 'child porn' or 'kiddie porn' and seen them used in the newspapers and on TV. These are very offensive terms to the Phoenix community and most decent-minded people.

Why? Because the word 'porn' suggests a legitimate commercial enterprise and a consent that simply does not exist in this arena. These images are indecent or obscene crime-scene photographs. They are photographic evidence of sex crimes against children. You would never call a picture of a dead person 'corpse porn' or images of a burglary 'theft porn'.

Abusers say it is a victimless crime, that it's a sort of harmless virtual methadone fix to help them keep their hands off the real thing. Others say the images are 'art' and that the children are nothing more than ink on paper or dots on a screen. The children in the pictures say that the images feel like a life sentence of exploitation and victimisation all of their own.

Unluckily for us, the term 'child porn' is so frequently used that we have to admit that the paedophiles did a very good job of rebranding what is a heinous crime against children into something bordering on socially acceptable. It happened in a flash. Just as a wider knowledge of this crime was starting to gain some momentum, before you could say, 'Please don't call it "child porn"', it had already become the headline-grabbing term – internationally embraced.

For our part, we have a worldwide struggle on our hands to turn back the tide on this one. We've tried to get the press to stop using the phrase, but it's not a battle we're likely to win in a hurry.

That said, the likes of the BBC's Jeremy Vine started things rolling for us by agreeing to never use the term again in his work. Thank you, Jeremy. Even the Justice Minister Jack Straw banned the use of this phrase throughout his department.

Getting the world to understand that words like 'kiddie' or 'child porn' are deeply offensive is going to be a tough one, but we live in hope. It's that kind of war of words we find ourselves fighting day after day.

Another example is how child abusers hijacked the word 'paedophile' right out from the English dictionary to help them distance themselves from the likes of 'nonce', 'beast' and 'child molester'. In most dictionaries, the word 'paedophile' means a person who loves children, not a person who sexually abuses them. It was the child molesters who chose the word 'paedophile'. They did this to try and legitimise their behaviour. Fortunately, they lost that one. The public simply used the word 'paedophile' to mean 'nonce', 'beast' and 'child molester'. In response, the paedophiles are currently trying out a new label. They're calling themselves 'child-attracted adults'. You couldn't make it up, could you?

Another example of the way our work is misrepresented by the world at large is when we read about female paedophiles. When the press talk about male teachers abusing their pupils, the language they use is always clear and emphatic: 'Pervert Teacher Commits Sex Crime Against Child.' Compare that to articles about female paedophile teachers, which they tend to say things like, 'Teacher and Pupil in Love Affair.' You can see how the words used change the way you think about the crime and how you respond to it. The knock-on effect is that the victims of female paedophiles tend to get less help, while female paedophiles get lighter sentences than their male counterparts.

We know that this thinking is reflective of our society, but the press seem locked down and reluctant to even call women offenders 'paedophiles', a reluctance that is evident in the likes of the Myra Hindley, Rose West and Tanya French cases.

Maybe it's time we all took a moment to look at the language we use and see if changes can be made to make victims feel less discriminated against.

Not long after Charles, we came across a case involving a little girl called Becky. There were a few problems with this case, like the way the police treated Becky. When they asked her to go over her statement – which involved recounting deeply distressing sexual abuse – they asked her to do so in a public place, with strangers walking and driving past her. The police were seriously failing in this case to obtain the best possible evidence, but they were also failing Becky.

The case itself was not unusual in so far as the mother married a man who sexually abused his stepdaughter from a very young age and into her late teens. The paedophile isolated the mother and child from the rest of their family, and isolated Becky from her older brothers and sisters. The mother eventually moved into Becky's bedroom and Becky was moved into her stepfather's bed to give him free rein.

Although Becky was never physically kept in a cellar, the emotional jail that her stepfather had made for her (aided, of course, by her own mother) was enough to keep her trapped until she was eighteen years old.

When a paedophile secures privileged and trusted access to a child as a family member – as Becky's stepfather did – they are able to groom the child from a very young age into enduring all kinds of abuse. This grooming can trap victims for years – well into adulthood. What paedophiles do is exploit the situation by continuing to abuse the step- or adopted child until just after they reach the legal age of consent. This way, if they're ever caught, the offender can simply claim the relationship was legal and consensual. This muddies the legal waters when it comes to trying to secure a criminal conviction and prejudices the legal system against victims who are not blood relatives. If you are a blood-related victim, then you never have to argue consent; if you are not blood-related, you often have to *prove* you did not consent.

The Becky case prompted us to campaign for a change in the law. We say the current incest law should be broadened to include step- and adopted children. The law at present clearly protects children in blood-related families from the perverted interest of those wishing to exploit their positions of trust, but does not do the same for step- or adopted children, certainly not in equal measures.

We want to change the law so that if you have ever parented a child under the legal age of consent, you are barred for life from ever marrying that child or from having a sexual relationship with them. We call this our LA Phoenix Law.

While we fought for all of these changes, we continued to work on changing the general discrimination suffered by victims at the hands of the system. We were also fighting specific battles against specific discrimination with organisations like the Criminal Injuries Compensation Authority, who for example still refuse to recognise or compensate victims of child sexual abuse that was perpe-trated by someone living as a member of the family before the mid-1970s.

We kept fighting. At the same time, we continued working to launch our RARE Retreat. Making calls, drafting letters, sending emails, drawing up wish lists and making plans.

39

The RARE Retreat was to be a set of buildings. We even had a specific site in mind. It would be a place of healing and learning. At the site, a countryside setting – it is a retreat, after all – we'd have advocates, legal experts, psychologists, counsellors and practical support workers: dedicated professionals, passionate about child protection and victim support, who would develop a template of care with the victims that could eventually be rolled out across the country.

As a victim, if you came to the retreat, you'd normally be brought by the police. There, you'd be able to give your statement in relaxed and safe surroundings, and once you'd finished doing that, the police would leave the retreat and you'd be able to take advantage of the facilities. We'd help you make sense of your experience. We'd give you the signposts you needed to guide you through the ordeal to come.

As a child protector, you would be brought to the RARE Retreat through your work, to one of the many seminars put together to share the knowledge and information gathered by the RARE team to help the professionals work with and better support the victims.

So, in October 2007, we launched the campaign for the RARE Retreat. It was never going to be easy. We couldn't do what others fundraisers could do to promote our causes. We didn't, for example, have a puppy dog to show people, or a before-and-after shot to tug on people's heartstrings. As usual, we had all the typical prejudices to overcome.

We never wanted RARE to be an official charity. We had tried this before, back in the days when we were fighting to keep Phoenix Survivors alive. There were a few problems, but the main ones for us were losing our independence, and the amount of money it costs to set up, run and maintain a registered charity before you can raise money for your cause.

Back when we'd been trying to set up the Phoenix Survivors charity, we had begun to realise something about the process. I discovered that paedophiles were registering themselves as charities. What sort of charities? The sort that are involved with children. This intelligence came to us via victims who alerted us to the fact that it was going on. Sure enough, when we did a bit of digging, it turned out to be true.

So we contacted the Charities Commission to say, 'We understand that you have a Child Protection Policy regarding charities and that you will vet anyone who wishes to set up a charity for children?'

Absolutely, we were told, of course.

Good, we said, excellent. It's reassuring to know that strict checks are in place to prevent paedophiles from setting up as a children's charity.

But of course Sara and I were going through the process of setting ourselves up as a charity. We had the forms in front of us and we studied them. There on the form we saw the rigorous process. It consisted of a box you had to tick, which isn't 'a check', no matter how you look at it.

So we got in touch with the *Daily Mirror*. With them we picked the name of a notorious paedophile and we filled in the forms in his name, for a fictitious charity called Give Kids a Break. And even though this man was currently in prison for hoarding images of child sex abuse and would be on the Sex Offenders Register for life, we named him as the charity's child-protection officer, in charge of personally taking abused children abroad on holiday breaks.

Application accepted.

Of course, as soon as the story came out, the Charities Commission promised an overhaul of the rules and thanked the *Daily Mirror* for bringing the loophole to their attention. As a result of that, these days you have to have a CRB check to set up as a children's charity.

Not that it helped *us* in our application, of course, and what was especially galling at the time was how easy it was for a convicted sex offender to register as a charity, when for us it was proving more difficult. Phoenix Survivors had been a charity for about a month when we decided to close it down. We didn't want to revisit those options and preferred instead to launch the RARE appeal as an independent not-for-profit organisation.

We knew it would be tough going, so we braced ourselves for the long haul. We began making enquiries. We went on TV and talked about it to immaculately turned-out hosts. We spoke to ministers, to the National Lottery and to all the usual suspects. Most people made all the right noises and things looked positive, but as we joined the ranks of all those looking for funding for a very good cause, we began to realise just how tough this was going to be. We needed to raise £3 million (or, as Sara and I would call it, 'telephone-numbers money') to get RARE up and firmly on its feet. We knew we could do it if we were given the opportunity. Sara and I wanted to help set up the RARE team, help develop the template of care and advocate where it was needed. We wanted to be a strong voice at the heart of RARE and help the professionals ensure it revolved round the victims' needs.

We were doing all we could, wherever we could, in between everything else we were doing, to campaign for the RARE appeal, but as always there was work to do back at our virtual office.

40

While we waited to hear whether we would receive funding for our RARE appeal, our caseload continued to increase. Still our fingers stayed in the dam.

We were contacted by a girl named Stacey, a scared nineteen-year-old single mum who had been abused by her own father for as long as she could remember. For years and years she had lived with the abuse, not wanting to alert the authorities for fear of getting her father into trouble. She was in so deep, so trapped by her abusive father, that she had his children.

The first baby was born when she was aged fifteen, at which point she ran away to live in a hostel. At the time, she was having an on-off relationship with an eighteen-year-old she'd met at the local benefits office. She'd lied to him about her age and they had sex in a caravan parked on his grandparents' land. The abuse by her father continued. She told her boyfriend that there was another man in her life – another boyfriend, who had threatened to hurt her if she left him. That way, she managed to keep the secret. She became pregnant by her father again.

In all, she had four babies. Each time she became pregnant she would split up with her boyfriend, claiming her violent other 'boyfriend' was suspicious. The truth, of course, was that she couldn't bear to give birth to another one of her father's children in front of the man she really loved.

The world at large assumed that the babies belonged to the eighteen-year-old boyfriend; he assumed they belonged to her fake boyfriend.

She kept her babies away from her father, but as they grew up, he started to put pressure on her to see them. She wanted help but was scared that social services would take her babies away. In desperation she turned to us.

We gave it to her straight: 'If you can't stop your father from abusing you, how do you expect to prevent him abusing your own children?'

If she wanted to keep her kids, we told her, then she needed help.

Accepting this was the only way she could stop her children being abused by her father – from suffering the same fate as her. Because that's the way paedophiles operate: if allowed, they will move from one generation to the next.

We talked for hours about her fears, how keeping all those secrets was killing her. Although she hated how they came into the world, she clearly loved her children. They were so much more to her than just her father's dirty little secrets.

She told us she was sure she was the only one he had abused (where had we heard that one before?). We told her – very gently – that this was probably a lie, at which point she began to realise that her little sister and *her* children might be in the same bad place.

She and her sister talked to each other. They screamed at each other, cried with each other, then forgave each other. Finally, after many more hours of talking, they went together to the authorities and – in their words – dropped a paedophile bomb on their families. It turned out that one of her sister's two children had been fathered by her dad. Of Stacey's own children, two turned out to be her father's; the other two had been fathered by her much-loved boyfriend.

Social services did initially take the children away, but after a full investigation and assessments they were returned to their loving mother, along with a team of family support workers and health visitors.

Her father was sent to jail and she rekindled her relationship with her first love. He had loved her all along and told her that he would help her to break the abuse cycle and bring up all four children as his own.

Today, they are a strong and loving family. They still get help and support when they need it, and although the dark days are long past them, they have never forgotten how bad things were and still can't believe how much better life is without Stacey's father's dirty secrets and abuse poisoning their lives.

In the end, the cycle of abuse was ended because they had the strength to tell.

It's easy enough to write about finding the strength to tell, but how do you do it in reality? The thing to remember is that paedophiles are essentially cowards. They target the smallest and most vulnerable, which basically tells you more about them than they ever want you to know.

There are many emotional tricks paedophiles play on their victims and those they groom. One fairly clever one is this idea that you will destroy their lives if you tell.

Telling doesn't destroy lives; it destroys lies. If you or your family are being forced to live a lie, it will undermine you all. The lie could break you up, but not the truth. The truth hurts; there is no lie about that. It is an agony for all those involved and it will change everything, but it is worth it, as it will, in the end, change things for the better.

Tricking victims into believing that 'telling' destroys lives is a crucial part of keeping the secret and therefore the abuse going. The paedophile's life wasn't destroyed when the victim first told; it was destroyed when the paedophile first abused them.

There is a life after paedophile crime and it could be a good one if you have the will to make it so, but there are one or two things we think you should know. Firstly, what do you do if there is a paedophile in your family? There are only a few occasions when most families will temporarily set aside any grievances and act as one, like weddings, funerals and the issue of child protection. So whether it is a mother, brother, friend or foe, the first thing to do is call a family meeting. The next thing to do is ask for a meeting with the police. Stay calm and keep it respectful, as in this meeting you will be told the details of the paedophile's convictions.

As a family, the first thing to accept is that all those who come into contact with the offender will, to some degree, be groomed, and you will have to work through your feelings about that. Professional emotional debriefing can help with severe cases, but essentially you just need to do the opposite of what a paedophile needs. So don't keep secrets from each other, make sure you talk to each other, and work together as a team to manage the risk to your family. Have the 'what's private talk' with the children and, where it's appropriate, name the people you're worried about.

Never, no matter what they say, give the paedophile any alone time with children, day or night. Paedophiles normally identify and target the more isolated members, then act to further isolate them. Don't allow it. If you need help, support or guidance, ask for it, and remember, information and communication are everything. Write a family letter to the paedophile's probation officer (to discuss with the paedophile) explaining that you all know the truth, that the family are acting as one to prevent re-offending, that there are new rules for any supervised contact with adults or children from the family and that there will be consequences if the rules are broken – broken rules are always reported to the probation officer.

41

Kevin was just fourteen. His dad was away fighting in the army, and he had a distant relationship with his mum, who worked long hours. As a result, he was what we once used to call a latchkey kid. He was bored at home and unfortunately he did what bored kids do – he got into mischief.

Kevin went online. This was in the very early days of the Internet, when, for adults, it was a magical fun box to the whole wide world. For children, it was a forbidden magic box of fun that everyone was talking about – the one with all the best games on it. In those days, there was very little in the way of online rules, policing or proof-of-age policies.

Rather than go on suitable sites, Kevin secretly started trawling adult dating sites. He signed up to one and said in his profile that he was an eighteen-year-old. He named his village and listed his hobbies as fishing and clubbing.

He was making a very, very big mistake.

To him, it was a game, an experiment, a way to relieve the boredom. Perhaps he even thought it would be a bit of a laugh, a wind-up. But he was way, way out of his depth. Back then, the Internet was swamped with XXX and little else. In such a predatory environment, a child would be very easily spotted and targeted by online sex offenders.

That is exactly what happened. One of the site's users, called Jay, started talking to Kevin. He lived just two villages away, he said. He also loved fishing and he was also eighteen.

After six months of talking – Jay constantly probing for more and more information – Kevin admitted his real age. At first, Jay pretended to be shocked. He claimed he felt let down that he'd been lied to. Kevin talked him round though, and in the end they both agreed that Jay would forgive Kevin for lying and that they would still go fishing together, as previously suggested. See what he did there?

When they met at a deserted fishing lake, Jay turned out to be a forty-year-old man called Jack. He told Kevin he was Jay's father, come to ensure Kevin wasn't a weirdo, and Kevin went along with it. Jack took Kevin into his fishing tent and raped him. Kevin didn't say no; he didn't know how to.

After his ordeal, Kevin went home but didn't tell his mum what had happened, frightened that she'd be furious with him for going on the site, for arranging the meeting, for putting himself in such danger. Neither could he tell his father. Instead, he was forced to keep what had happened a secret. Worse, he would see Jack: the one thing Jack hadn't lied about was that he lived not far away, so they saw one another again on the one and only bus route through the villages. Kevin was forced into committing a sex act on Jack behind the bus-stop. After that, he became too afraid to take the bus, so he started skipping school. Bored at home, he went back online and in no time was being bombarded with messages from Jack.

It was then that Kevin emailed us. He would not identify himself at first, despite the fact that he was in very real danger from Jack. Plus, he was experiencing some distressing physical symptoms. We told him to tell his mother, to see his doctor and get checked for STDs, but he wouldn't – he was just too afraid.

So we asked our Phoenix web ferrets to investigate both Kevin and Jack's online activity. It wasn't our first online grooming case, but we were all shocked at how much private information Kevin had put on the Internet.

Then one day I was speaking to Sara when Kevin sent another message. He said Jack was outside his house and he'd brought a friend.

I replied, begging him to tell his mother.

'No,' he said. He was still too frightened. Besides, she was out.

'Do you want me to tell her?' I asked.

'Yes,' he said eventually.

I called his mum, who rang the police and dashed home to save her son. There was a tense fifteen minutes as we waited for the police to arrive, but they got there before she did and she arrived to find a house full of coppers. And Kevin, in tears but thankfully safe.

They questioned Jack, of course, who claimed the sexual encounters were with a consensual adult. As Kevin had lied about his age and the evidence of this was all over his mum's computer, there was nothing they could do. It was one person's word against another's. For our part, we helped mum and son become friends again, and we started working harder still to bring about online grooming laws and CEOP – the Child Exploitation and Online Protection Centre.

42

Picture a room. Along one wall is a bank of computers, most of them dormant, their screensavers swirling lazily. Just one is active, and in front of it sits a police officer, his hands moving over the keyboard, guiding the mouse. *Click. Click. Click.*

Suddenly he jerks that little bit straighter in his seat. 'OK,' he says, 'I've got something here.'

Adjacent chairs are pulled back. Other officers join him, pulling keyboards close, yanking headsets towards them. Somewhere a child is being abused. The abuse could be being planned, discussed or even broadcast online via a webcam. The police have at most an hour in which to gather as much information as they can before the digital trail goes cold. The room is within the bowels of a building in South London and is the headquarters of CEOP.

It's not all thanks to Phoenix that this room exists, but we did as much as anyone to wave the flag. We were there at its inception. And here's the funny thing: my involvement owes a lot to an unnamed paedophile who wrote to tell me that he was about to masturbate over a picture of me as a child. By doing that, he unwittingly helped create one of the world's most effective weapons in the war against him and his kind. Let me explain.

When we first came online with Phoenix Survivors, one

thing quickly became apparent to me, and it was this: the Internet belonged to *them*. This was some years ago, obviously, before the web was colonised by big businesses, and let's face it, it's an altogether more civilised place now. In its early years, however, the Internet was the habitat of a very different beast altogether. Without anybody noticing, a massive base of sex offenders had developed. Where once they had just used the post, they now used the post *and* the Internet. We called them the 'online sex-offender community' – the OSC for short – and, for a while, the Internet belonged to them.

Make no mistake, behind every OSC username is a real inhuman being living in the real world. People sometimes look at you like you're mad when you tell them there's an online sex-offender community, but there is, and you can virtually pinpoint its creation to one moment in time. That moment was when the Internet went live to the general public. As soon as the digital airways were activated, the sex-offender community set about publishing thousands of pervert how-to websites. They would collect together and target 'child-friendly' websites cruising for potential victims. These pervert how-to websites tended to be text-only sites that published links to the illegal stuff and were, by all accounts, the information backbone of the OSC. They may not have had any images on these how-to sites, but by exploiting the freedom-of-speech laws, they published indescribable pro-paedophile rubbish that left you wondering how the hell they were getting away with so flagrantly inciting others to commit sex crimes against children.

There was no such thing as an online police force, so

if you were a target of the OSC and wanted help, protection or justice, you were in for a terrible surprise. Go to your local police station and you'd have been told, 'Not our patch.' Police forces worked in terms of districts and areas; they had maps on their office walls so they knew if it was their crime or if it belonged to the force next door. And cyber-space wasn't on the local Ordnance Survey.

Furthermore, nobody could agree whose responsibility it was to police the Internet or to pay for policing the Internet. It had to be somebody's responsibility, of course. We just didn't know *who* at that point: it was a new place, jurisdiction had yet to be decided, let alone policed.

Trouble was, while everybody was squabbling, the OSC were becoming fully mobilised. They were inventing and crafting the not-so-noble art of Internet grooming; they were setting up ever more pervert how-to websites, with advice on the legal rights of paedophiles and teaching each other the sort of things you can and can't say when you're trying to ensnare a young victim; they'd be discussing their interests as openly and with as much enthusiasm as Pink Floyd fans or golf enthusiasts were discussing theirs. Here at last was a place where they felt comfortable, and it was open season.

This is what we found when we came online as Phoenix. Thanks to information passed to us by our web ferrets, we found that the OSC – made up of paedophiles, their facilitators and their supporters – had indeed effectively hijacked huge sections of the web and had turned it into a virtual no-man's land – where most trained bastards would fear to tread, let alone angels.

But that wasn't even the half of it. The OSC had long been busy setting up countless blogs and newsgroups representing and facilitating every department of their depraved 'dark market' and its perverted worldwide consumer base.

Here was a space where paedophiles no longer felt like social pariahs, a place where they could validate themselves into a complete froth. In fact, they were telling each other that it was the rest of the world that was out of step with them, that they were comparable to the homosexuals of yesteryear, despised and cast out for their sexual preferences, but now legally and socially protected. As far as they were concerned, it was just a matter of time before they too were accepted as a legal sexual minority with the right to abuse any child they wanted to. We know. We know.

Paedophilia and homosexuality have never had any connection with each other. One is all about two age-appropriate adults consenting to sex; the other is about an adult sexually abusing and exploiting a child. This is just a taste of how they can twist anything to suit their thinking.

It's the same kind of thinking that has led to them setting up their own political party in Holland. The Brotherly Love, Freedom and Diversity Party (PNVD) sparked outrage around the world when it began announcing a stomach-churning manifesto, including lowering the age of consent to twelve and legalising child pornography and sex with animals. They wanted to break taboos and fight intolerance, they said. Paedophilia should be discussed by one and all and, yes, even *practiced*, so that children shouldn't be curious about sex. At the same time they tried to set up a political party over here in the UK.

OK, deep breath. It never got off the ground. Thank God for small mercies as it didn't go further than just an idea. But even so, you can clearly see what these people are playing at. What they're trying to do is legitimise something that's so disgusting and unnatural and evil it doesn't bear thinking about. They're online right now talking about how hard done by they are. Really. They are. They will be talking about how they are persecuted, how they're martyrs.

In this world, it was us who were the underdogs, and we were inundated with the most appalling abuse and harassment imaginable. Every perverted online stalker seemed to be targeting our inbox with their most disgusting imaginations. The OSC blogs were buzzing with unspeakably disturbing posts about us, threatening to abuse us, our families, our loved ones and even our supporters. We were warned (threatened) in no uncertain vile-mouthed terms that when it comes to the Internet, we were on their virtual turf and we were not welcome, to say the very least. We were shocked at first, but we knew they were trying to scare us off and that we needed to keep our wits about us, so we stayed calm and pushed on. We took a firm stand against the OSC and started closing down their information backbone, their pervert 'how to' websites. It was then that they turned their fully focused attention upon us and did all they could to put the frighteners on us.

The message was clear: they didn't like what we were doing or what we had to say, and we should shut up and go away.

We argued (back in the days when we used to respond) that we didn't need their permission, nor were we seeking it, and that we had the same human rights and freedom of speech as everyone else.

They dismissively argued, not in their virtual world we didn't.

We responded, so no different than in the real world, then?

They didn't reply.

We wondered if it was a battle we could win though. The OSC had been growing in numbers, evolving their community at lightning speed. They were now well past being an active online community of like-minded perverts who generally worked well together; they had become a more sleek, organised, funded instrument of unprecedented bloody horror that was leaving millions of child victims in its terrifying wake.

We began to speak up about it. What we said was, we need somewhere to report all this stuff. Here you have the Internet and it's like *Mad Max* in there, and something needs to be done about it. We need one central law-enforcement unit that will take responsibility for all this stuff. What we really wanted was not just all the police forces from across the UK to come together, but forces from across the world.

We had a sympathetic ear in the amazing Jim Gamble, a senior police officer. Let me tell you a little about him: a natural born child protector, there are so many children who won't be hurt by paedophiles because of the work that he and his teams have done (and still do) to protect children. To the victims of child sexual abuse and exploitation from around the world, he is a hero, an absolute hero. Please someone give this man, and his team, knighthoods because they have been responsible for some of the most outstanding child-protection work ever done in this field.

As deputy director-general of the UK's National Crime Squad, Jim had worked on the Operation Cathedral team, which was responsible for taking down one of the first high-profile online paedophile rings, the Wonderland Club, in 1998. Wonderland had 180 members in 21 countries and at the time was seen as being a major, organised ring. It was at a time when only about 9 to 12 per cent of people in the UK had Internet access – a drop in the ocean compared to today's numbers.

Five years later, over half the country was online and Jim found himself heading up another major operation – Operation Ore. The online numbers had risen dramatically in the years since Operation Cathedral. As a result of Operation Avalanche, the UK police were given a list of – wait for it – over 7,000 names, which triggered what came to be known as Operation Ore.

In brief, an American couple, Thomas and Janice Reedy, set up a website, Landslide, that provided a portal to every kind of child sexual abuse and exploitation imaginable. The website's computers collected the details of all those who traded in this dark market. So when the Reedys were caught, the police found a list of thousands of potential sex offenders from around the world whose credit cards and Internet accounts had been used to pay for things like indecent images of children.

The Landslide list triggered Operation Ore and it has since been reported that, beyond the multiple convictions and sex offender intelligence gathering it engendered, Operation Ore has more importantly led to the rescue of

132 children from hands-on abusers. But something else seemed to happen as well. It seemed to alter society's view on whether indecent images were art or crime.

Now please don't misunderstand us here. We feel that it is absolutely proper for parents to photograph their children's lives, including such pictures as kids in paddling pools being chased around by mum or dad pretending to be scary 'cold water' hose monsters in the back garden on a hot summer's day. Like most normal people, however, we believe that such candid family pictures should be kept private, except that is for use by parents to embarass their children when they bring the first girlfriend or boyfriend home, in the far distant future, but otherwise completely private, both the for the individual's sake and that of the greater good. Until a child reaches adulthood, parents and/or legal guardians are in charge of protecting them from exploitation, but we feel this duty of protection is all too easily signed away by less scrupulous parents and guardians, some of whom have been happy to sell compromising images of their children. Failure to legally challenge such parents over the years resulted in a shocking social tolerance of this particular crime, to such a degree that vile indecent images of children were actually considered a kind of art and not a crime against the child.

Before Operations Cathedral and Ore, there was indeed a great deal of legal ambiguity about indecent images of children, and consequently the victims of indecent images rarely saw the inside of a courtroom. So, no legal protection. This ambiguity was of course being exploited to death by the sex-offender community in general, according to whom this was a victimless crime, art, just ink on paper. The Ore and Cathedral teams helped the public to connect with the real living breathing children trapped inside these indecent images and, once that happened, it crystallised public opinion on this whole issue. The general consensus was that indecent images of children were serious crimes against children and from then on everything seemed to change for the better.

To handle the sheer number of investigations created by Operation Ore, Jim called for the formation of a unit called the Paedophile Online Investigation Team. When the operation was over, however, he knew the police needed something bigger, and with more reach, to help combat this abusive and fast-growing crime.

We needed a global police force dealing solely with child sex abuse and exploitation, he concluded. We couldn't have agreed more. Fired up by the idea, he organised a three-day meeting in London with police agencies, government officials and child protectors from around the world, and presented it to them. They wanted to tackle the crime but couldn't commit the resources, so were resistant and seemed about to say no. On the last night of the conference, Jim called me.

'They're not doing it, Shy. They're not going with it. They have another set of priorities – understandable priorities, but I think they need to hear from you.'

A vision of the future swam into my head. A future where the Internet continued to be monopolised by paedophiles, where police forces were *still* not speaking to each other, where there was still no central repository for information. I couldn't until that point imagine it getting worse than it already was, but the thought of it filled me with utter dread.

'Will you come and talk to them?' said Jim.

I nearly screamed out loud. My mind was racing and arguing with itself about never going out and meeting strangers and what would I say and this is what we have wanted for years . . .

'Jim, I don't . . . I have . . . I wouldn't even know what to say.'

'Just say anything,' he said. 'Just talk to them like you talk to me. Tell them what it was like, anything. Can you just talk to them?'

'Let me think about it,' I said. 'Call me back in ten.'

He rang off and I did as promised: I thought about it.

I sat there thinking about the chatrooms, and the webcams, the pervert 'how to' sites where paedophiles talked about the 'meat menu' or their 'little friends' – and that's when they were being polite.

Then I thought about all those OSC emails.

One of the ways in which I was abused as a child was when I was photographed and filmed being sexually abused and exploited. Such indecent images have an infinite shelf-life as a valuable swap-or-sell commodity among the sex-offender community and were apparently circulated around the dark market for decades. When the Internet entered the public domain, sex offenders the world over burned out a mountain of computer scanning equipment translating their personal libraries into online swap shops or digital paedophile pounds to spend in the ever-increasing online dark market.

As far as I know, neither of the films taken of me have

ever come to light – certainly I've never received any evidence they have – and for that I can at least be thankful. As I understand it, however, some of the indecent pictures are out there. One of the reasons I know this is because the OSC write and tell me so. I once wrote a piece explaining that the smile I was forced to wear in those indecent images was not real. This seemed to irritate the OSC no end. I had an email from one member boasting that he'd just downloaded an image of me as a child and my smile looked real enough to him and he was off to have a . . . Well, you know the rest.

I thought about that for a while, how that made me feel. It's difficult to put the feeling into words, but 'invaded' would be one. 'Violated' another. 'Hacked off' two more. 'Not prepared to sit around and do nothing about it' were even more. How dare they try to use a crime committed against me when I was too little to fight back, to victimise me as an adult when I *am* big enough to fight back!

When Jim Gamble rang me back, I knew I would help. I thought, we have needed an online police force for so long now, so if there was anything I could do to help make it happen, I had to try. So I made up my mind to go to that meeting. I took a few of those OSC emails and something else I'd been sent, and before I knew it, I found myself in this very grand room sitting at a huge table shaking like a bloody leaf at the thought of standing up and talking to all of these people. I couldn't eat the meal because I was too busy thinking about what the hell I was going to say.

Suddenly, there I was standing up to talk to them. When I opened my mouth to speak, the words just came out of me. The shaking stopped and I explained how the Internet had become the paedophiles' place, not theirs, and that if they wanted to reclaim that place, then they had to do something about it; they needed to take charge. If they could just embrace the Internet as the OSC had done, they could use it to catch the predators.

Then I told them my story. I told them how it felt to be photographed, how it felt to know that people were still looking at images taken of me all those years ago. I described my feelings of invasion and violation. I told them what it felt like being the victim of a crime that never stops being committed and what a life sentence that can sometimes be.

I told them how they were the hope of hundreds of thousands of children just like me waiting for them to come to their rescue. I showed them some of the emails the OSC had sent to me and asked them to take the lead in the fight against them. And then I thanked them for coming to hear me.

It reduced them to tears. I can't say it was *exactly* the desired effect. I mean, I wanted to reach them, of course, but not scar them. I wasn't complaining though. Not then, knowing I'd got through to them, and not afterwards when they all came up to pledge support for what would become VGT, the Virtual Global Taskforce.

In a nutshell, the VGT is an international alliance made up of law-enforcement agencies around the globe. Their aim is to fight child abuse online, to make the Internet a safer place, to identify, help and locate children at risk, whether these are kids in photos or being groomed, and to get the abusers and bring them to book.

But the VGT was only one step. The government –
together with local practitioners, the police, industry and
children's charities – realised that more had to and could
be done. Vitally, they also recognised that what was needed
was a completely different way of working – a way that
would be holistic and that would bring all interested sectors
together.

The answer was the Child Exploitation and Online
Protection Centre, or CEOP as it is affectionately known.
Set up in 2006, this was an organisation like no other
multi-agency child-protection team before them. Its
members were cutting-edge, the best in their field; uniquely,
they were child protectors the public could actually get
behind, support and even help to evolve. In no time at
all, by adopting a truly partnership-driven approach, they
were making major inroads into the active OSC.

In one case, based on a posting from an OSC networking
site (from someone claiming to have his children up for
sale to the highest paedophile bidder), CEOP managed
to identify the account holder responsible for the posting,
stop him and remove his children to a permanent place
of safety. They were so good at what they did that they
were only limited by how well other agencies worked
together and by how much the government was prepared
to fund them.

Both the VGT and CEOP have excellent websites and
I urge you to go and look at them. When you do – when
you see these two huge entities fighting – spare a thought
for the poor old paedophile who helped make it happen,
who wrote to me to gloat about the fact that he'd just
downloaded my picture. Think about who might be

gloating now, now that CEOP is a big, powerful child-protection centre of excellence that is recognised the world over.

In 2007, it was responsible for dismantling six organised paedophile rings and arresting more than 300 suspected child sex offenders. CEOP has infiltrated the world of the child sex abuser. It uses Internet and technical know-how to go deep into the computer networks of child sex abusers and crack them wide open. It has a behavioural analyst unit to look at how child sex offenders think and act. It has child protectors whose job it is to feed hundreds of thousands of indecent images of children into a highly sophisticated face-recognition software unit developed by Microsoft to help identify victims and offenders. It has an education programme – thinkuknow – that like no other is driven by law enforcement and has now reached over 4 million children with lesson plans that look to keep them safe online.

CEOP has officers whose job it is to pose as possible victims in chatrooms, to try and weed out the predators (paedo-phishing, we call it). It has officers whose job it is to infiltrate OSC sites, posing as paedophiles. Can you imagine what these guys have to go through? CEOP also publishes an online list of most-wanted offenders. It works with other police forces across the world. They have very quickly become the best in their field. A national centre of true excellence, sitting at the hub of UK policing, sharing best practice, intelligence and bespoke services like never before.

And we're not just saying this because we were involved in its inception; it really is one of the best child-protection centres in the world – respected internationally. Anyone who has a child-protection problem can call upon them. The Madeleine McCann case, for example: after the local authorities failed to deploy a suitable child-abduction policy when Maddie disappeared, CEOP were eventually called in to see if anything useful could be salvaged to help find her.

CEOP work with the local police force to bring them up to speed on offender-profiling. Does this match your crime? Why do paedophiles do what they do? These are the places they like to do it. Have you had any other cases like this? Has anyone who holidayed in the same areas ever complained of any child-protection issues either here or back where they live? Can we help you build a crime file so that you're looking in the right direction for the right people?

It's a sad fact that it doesn't always work. In Maddie's case, we're still looking – we're always looking.

In the meantime, we continue to work hand in hand with CEOP wherever we can. So, for example, a Phoenix web ferret might report that 'Someone is posting on one of the pervert how-to websites today calling himself "God's gift".'

This is a take from a well-known username we already know of called 'Son of God', as you may remember from Julian Sher's recent book on this subject called *One Child at a Time*. 'Son of God' is sometimes used in homage to a major paedophile based in the States who called himself GOD, which stood for 'Galactic Overlord Duplicate' and which sounds like something a lovable video-games nerd might call himself.

Only GOD was about as far away from a lovable video-games nerd as you can imagine. He traded in images of children being forced into sexual acts, thousands upon thousands of them, in a chatroom called Kiddypics and Kiddyvids. He was eventually arrested as part of a major international operation called Operation Wickerman.

It was online creatures like this who inspired one very special police officer called Detective Sergeant Paul Gillespie to send an email to Bill Gates which basically said 'I'm a police officer and you're a techie and I need your help'. Bill Gates put the head of Microsoft (Canada) in touch with him. They worked together to develop a wonderful piece of software called the Child Exploitation Tracking System (CETS), a free tool provided internationally by Microsoft to help law-enforcement officers find, track down, arrest and lock up paedophiles in our societies. The tool has since been deployed in seven countries and has been used in more than 800 investigations.

CETS does many incredible things and we know it best as the online Digital Bloodhound. It can track offenders' usernames all over the web and send back intelligence reports to help the child protectors. Children around the world will forever be in debt to DS Gillespie and his child-protection teams for helping to make the Internet a safer place.

We have often heard it said that the Internet is nothing more than a giant paedophile-making machine, and that since it came online there has been an explosion in paedophile activity. We would argue that there were always this many paedophiles out there, and that although the Internet has indeed been fully exploited by paedophiles the world over, it has also helped to catch and stop more paedophiles than at any time in the history of child protection.

When the web first became available to the public, the paedophile community threw all secretive caution to the wind and started signing up to the various OSC websites, using their names and details. They fully believed one of the Internet's greatest myths: that those who use digital identities do so with untraceable anonymity. Wrong. For a start, every Internet-connectable gadget has its own digital fingerprint, its IP address, which transmits itself every time it logs on to the Internet. The fact is, in an online digital world, everything you do leaves a digital footprint recorded by someone somewhere. And yes, if you don't know what you are looking for it can be difficult, but when you do, it's a whole different story. There is no such thing as complete anonymity or untraceable digital footprints. For every scrambler, there is an unscrambler. For every virtual locked door, there are virtual locksmiths quite able to open it. This wasn't something the OSC seemed to understand and we were not about to tell them.

Because of the likes of CEOP, these days it's normally only ever a matter of time after you commit an online crime before the police are there in person knocking on your door with actual handcuffs.

This can only be a good thing, as in recent times the OSC has taken sexually abusing and exploiting children to a whole new, vile level: live pay-as-you-go webcasts. What happens is that paedophiles will sexually abuse a child on a webcam and broadcast it live to other paedophiles. Yes, really, this actually happens. More than that, they charge for this service, so eager paedophiles will feed money into an online bank account in order to see the abuse. Often, the abuser will take requests. It beggars belief, I know, but it goes on.

The OSC now have their web servers, their own media, expert and legal departments, their own political campaigners. They have become a true force to be reckoned with, and anybody who tries to stand up to them will receive the full glare of the most unwelcome attention.

Sara and I have watched many highly respected child protectors from across the board being publicly targeted and abused by the OSC. There is no doubt that we have been able to make some headway in the battle against them, but so much more needs to be done. We need a more active online police presence than ever before to stand any chance of stopping this new kind of OSC activity, but as with everything in this world that needs to be done, it all comes down to how much the powers that be are prepared to pay to get it done.

We can see for ourselves that CEOP, for example, needs an extra £10 million over and above what they ordinarily get in order to stay on the same battlefield as the OSC. It's £10 million now or £50 million later to mop up the mess for failing to act. Unfortunately, in the middle of a worldwide recession, in which every public service is facing previously unthinkable cuts, the OSC are rubbing their sticky little hands in gleeful anticipation, as they wait to see exactly how low child protection will feature in the social funding priority list.

43

Sara and I have been personally responsible for closing down many pervert how-to websites over the years. We do this simply by following the trail of digital breadcrumbs left by the Internet service provider. Once at their door, we advise them of what their services are being used for and by whom. Normally within a few hours the site will vanish. As you can imagine, this doesn't make Sara and I at all popular with the OSC.

Because we refused to cave in to these perverted cyber-stalking bullies, they stepped things up a notch. One of them nearly tricked me into appearing on a national news programme with him. At the last moment, I discovered who it was and cancelled. I later found out that the OSC had carefully planned the whole thing and were furious that it had failed.

Next, they turned their attention to attacking Sara and, worse still, Sarah. I can't repeat what was posted on the OSC blogs – it's just too distressing – but, not long after a rash of disgusting postings, the national news reported that flowers, allegedly sent by her murderer, had been left on Sarah's grave. Sara and her family were so upset they needed time out to recover.

Some time ago, I was voted 'Most Hated Female' by the online sex-offender community. Shortly after hearing about this, I put a little piece on the Phoenix site along the lines of 'I'm only disappointed it didn't come with a certificate.' About a week later, a certificate turned up.

That's one of the reasons I use a PO Box, not my real address, and why I have so many security measures in place on my computers. Let's just say the OSC like to keep in touch. (To give you an idea of the kind of email I receive: 'You're the worst sort of abuser there is on the planet, because what you do is teach children that the nice thing that just happened to them is bad. So who's really fucking abusing them, me or you?')

Truly, there are no depths that these people will not sink to. Did you know, for example, that at one time they had an online victims chart? You would no doubt recognise the names of the victims on it. It was a league table of their 'most-wanted' victims. Sick? Yes. But also legal. They'll publish stories on their sites of the things they'd like to do to victims. Real victims become the subject of sick and disturbing stories, but apparently the stories are fantasy, so that's OK. Again, freedom of speech and all that. Any attempt to stop them is met with screams of 'oppression by the mind police'.

Working with online child-protection agencies and our own web ferrets, Sara and I keep an eye on the OSC and alert the appropriate authorities if anything worrying comes up.

Of course, the paedophiles are always trying to come up with new ways to stay online, so the paedophiles have started setting themselves up as service providers. We just have to find new ways of bringing them down.

You want our advice when it comes to the Internet?

Don't think you're safe just because you're sitting in your bedroom at home. Even if you're curious about what's going on after reading this, don't go and do anything about that curiosity. You don't want to do that for two reasons. Firstly, when you click on a website, your interest in that site is registered by the person who owns the site. They capture your IP address – your computer's finger-prints, remember – and you really don't want to be a blip on some paedophile's radar, do you? Secondly, your interest may be logged by a CEOP bait site, and you really don't want that, either. Even *we* have to be incredibly careful if we're looking online. Often we'll ask out web ferrets to check out sites for us first, with the help of organisa-tions like the Internet Watch Foundation, because just as the police have protocols and rules about viewing inde-cent images of child sex abuse, so do we. Our policy is that we never do.

Don't assume your children are safe, either. Some alarming figures released in 2006 revealed that one in seventeen children is threatened or harassed on the Internet, one in five had been aggressively solicited sexually online in the past year, and only 27 per cent of the young people who encountered unwanted sexual material online told a parent or guardian.

We wanted to give parents a smart tool to help them watch over their children's online activity, to warn them if anyone was attempting to meet with or groom their children, so we joined forces with a software designer. He had developed a brilliant computer program that could monitor a child's online activity and trigger an email alert to the parents if their child was being bullied, sexually propositioned or groomed online. It could also block visitation to unwanted websites. We found that this kind of software was an excellent way of assisting and empowering parents. If your child uses the Internet, our strong advice is that along with things like anti-virus software, anti-grooming software should be loaded on to all computers before they are given access to the Internet.

44

As usual, Sara and I continued to juggle many campaigns. While working on the fight against the OSC, we continued trying to set up the RARE Retreat. The meeting that would decide its future was to take place at the Home Office building on Marsham Street in London. It came about the way these things usually do: by us raising the issue until at last we got someone to listen.

We'd already had a terrible knock-back. All the usual suspects had replied to say, 'Sorry – not this time.' The National Lottery had been the last to respond. The news came in a letter one day. I looked at it in my hand, saw the postmark, the logo and took a deep breath. This is it, I thought. This is the letter telling us we've got the money. I had visions of the RARE Retreat opening.

Five minutes later, the letter lay on the table by my side. I gazed at the computer. From the Skype window, Sara stared back, her face a reflection of mine.

'Those . . . idiots,' I said, at last. 'It's cheaper to help sooner rather than later.'

Sara shook her head, thinking the same thing – that we see victims out there in pain and one way or another that pain puts them into the system, which costs money. If the authorities just had a bit foresight, a bit of vision, then we could avoid some of that pain.

Sometimes it's as though the people who hold the purse strings want more complicated answers. They want the solution to be something that only fifty professors and thirty academics could possibly dream up. They can't see that the answer is right in front of their faces and that it's quite simple and sometimes even cheaper, but it's like anything – like climate change, for example – you need to spend a bit now. You need to make changes today in order to reap the benefits in the long term. That's just the way it is.

You want to take hold of their shoulders and shake them. Yes, it is going to sound extraordinarily expensive, but if we pay for the proper monitoring and management of sex offenders and the proper care and treatment of victims, then in ten years time it will cost you half as much. You'll have a lot less offending. But no. Instead? Nothing.

'They're never going to get it, are they?' I said.

'No, Shy, no.' Sara shook her head. She looked as tired and as beaten up as I felt.

We have a phrase we use to describe the victims of abuse who go without help because they have no other choice: the hardcore ignored. There are so many hardcore ignored out there. If they had an illness, with easily identifiable symptoms, like purple spots, then it would be a pandemic; we would see a lot of people on the streets with purple spots. One in four people, of about 70 million, have been affected by child sexual abuse. I would go further and say that there isn't a school in the country that doesn't have at least one victim in it. That I can say for sure.

Sara and I were both incredibly downhearted after our applications for funding were rejected. It was so frustrating. Just as we were beginning to lose heart, a ray of hope appeared on the horizon. We received a phone call asking whether we wished to attend a meeting with the first ever female home secretary, Jacqui Smith. She had heard about RARE and had asked if we could come and see her at the Home Office. Could we? We thought about it for all of half a second. Yes, we could. We'd see her in a spider-infested cave full of screaming strangers if we thought it might bring us closer to RARE.

The day came and I left the house, heart in mouth. I met up with Sara and we went to a restaurant opposite the Home Office and sat there for a while, drawing up battle plans. Both of us were wearing black and white: we have a rule that whenever we're at an official meeting we wear black and white – very businesslike, very serious. We sat there talking about our strategy. We know each other's strengths and weaknesses and had learned to take over from each other during meetings if one of us was flagging. If it involves lots of long words, then it's me. Short words, closer and quicker to the point, then Sara. We're both very, very good on details, but we have our specialist subjects. We're both good on the OSC, for example, but if you want to talk about the finer points of our proposed Anti-Victim Prejudice and Discrimination Law, then it's me. Details of Sarah's Law, then Sara. When these issues come up in meetings, then one of us will take a step back and let the other do the talking.

For this particular meeting, it was, 'You get her hair and I'll get her eyes.' Metaphorically speaking, of course.

Don't get us wrong – we take things seriously. If we didn't, we wouldn't be doing our job. Doing our job properly is key for us. A lot of people rely on us to get this right. We're lucky because we have a public profile, of sorts, which gets us through the door, but after that it is up to us. After that, it's all professional.

Jacqui Smith knew of Sara and me, and even knew about my agrosociophobia, so she had got her staff to ring and ask if there was anything they could do to make it easier for me. This is the Home Office. If they want eleven people in a meeting, then eleven people are going to be in that meeting whether I'm sweating buckets or not. Even so, I liked that she had cared enough to try and make it as easy for me as possible.

The mood as we sat in the restaurant was fearful, rather than nervous. Neither of us really suffers from nerves, although I do get concerned about my habit of 'blurting', which is saying out loud the things that most people keep to themselves. It's not to be confused with Tourette's, but the effect can sometimes be similar. If you're meeting with the home secretary, the last thing you want to be doing is blurting.

Will I blurt? Will I talk too much? Will I say the wrong things? Will I stammer? Will I simply stop dead? I've trained myself to stop talking if I begin to stammer, which means I worry less about sounding like a stuck record, but I run the risk of clamming up. Will I swear? Will I repeat myself? Blurters repeat themselves, so that's always a worry. Plus, blurters repeat themselves, so that's always a worry.

Sara and I generally hammer out what we want to say beforehand. On this occasion, we had five bullet points, which might as well have been tattooed on the insides of our eyelids we knew them so well. We often use that strategy – five bullet points. It gives you something to hang on to during the meeting, a lifebuoy to aim for if you feel you're sinking.

'How do you feel?' asked Sara.

'Oh God,' I said, knowing that she knew how I felt. 'I suppose I'm worried,' I continued, summarising, to spare her the full director's cut. 'I dunno. Nervous isn't the word, is it?'

She shook her head, understanding perfectly. Across the road was the Home Office. *The Home Office*. Of course we were a little on edge. We're just normal women. But for some horrific twists of Fate, we're actually quite average people. Believe it or not, the Home Office isn't our natural habitat.

'I suppose I'm worried we won't deliver,' I said, at last.

'Yeah, me too.'

'Anything else?' she asked.

'Yeah.'

'What?'

'You first.'

She grinned, crossed her arms and leaned across the table towards me. 'I'm bloody excited is what I am. The home secretary. *Us*. You know what, Shy? We've known for a long time now what it is that's broken. We can see what it is that needs to be fixed and we've got the answer. It feels like we've been working and waiting and fighting and crying and trying to plug that bloody big hole forever. Now, suddenly, we've been given the chance to prove we can do this.'

She had me virtually bouncing up and down in my seat.

'Oh God, we've been the rank outsiders for so long now Sar; do you really think they will help us do it!'

We'd got ourselves so psyched up, like a couple of pro-boxers before a fight, that we had to calm each other down because we were getting way too optimistic. We were imagining a future in which RARE was up and running. In fact, there was more than one RARE Retreat; there was an entire network of them. We had advocates and counsellors up and down the country and—

'OK,' said Sara, putting an end to the fantasising. 'Let's get back down to earth, shall we?'

'Bump.'

'Bump.'

'Let's go, babe.'

How crucial was this meeting? I wondered, as we nego-tiated the busy road across to the Home Office building. Pretty blimmin' crucial, was the answer. If we could get the government on board, it would bring us closer to all the bigger changes we were trying to make. Achieving that wasn't just an idle hope now, either. We had respect and profile. We were at the stage where the government could trust us with the kind of task ahead of us. And if they wouldn't give us the cash, then at least they might give us their support.

Our optimism was based on their positive feedback, on them giving us the impression that they were behind us. It's worth remembering, too, that our history with these guys went beyond simply agitating them to change legis-lation. When the government needed consultants on child-protection issues, they often called on the likes of us and we would work with them.

As we approached the building, I allowed myself to think, we've got their respect, their trust. They believe in our expertise. We've never before gone to them cap in hand, so it's not like we've always been asking for cash. Yes, I thought, this is our time.

45

The Home Office is very light, bright and modern. It's all glass – even the internal walls – so it has the impression of space. Some of it is open-plan. Other sections are divided up into offices used by *les grandes fromages*, and at the Home Office, the *fromages* don't get much more *grand* than Jacqui Smith.

Obviously we can't go into the security arrangements for the Home Office. Suffice to say, you get the sense they've scanned your DNA before you get to the security desk. As you make your way through, you're searched, scanned, sniffed and finally wafted to your destination in lifts that don't have buttons the way normal lifts do. Instead, the person escorting you scans something over a card-reader that tells the lift where to go. Then the doors close and the next time they open you're on the right floor. No 'Room for one more?' here. No worries about stopping at every floor. These are smart lifts. It means, of course, that if you don't have a card, you're stranded. This is the same anywhere you go in the building. No escort, no go.

Sara and I loved it, of course. Never dropping our professional and businesslike exterior, we nevertheless managed to communicate our excitement – in secret and in sign language.

'Are you sweating?' she whispered.

'No, I'm all right. How's my hair?'

'Your hair's fine.'

We were led up to the floor for the home secretary. More glass-walled offices. At the end was hers. We were ushered in. No sign of Jacqui yet.

Funny thing is, the view from her office sucks. For all I know, there may be a security reason for this, but I do remember thinking, Bummer, Jacqui – you don't seem to have the wonderful panoramic view of the city that everybody else has. Hers was probably the biggest office on the floor; that much was clear. Around it were conference rooms, but you had the impression that Jacqui's was the biggest.

Now the hyper-vigilance kicked in. I took in her chair and desk. I saw the computer, stickers, badges. In front of her desk was a seated area with a sofa and an easy chair. I don't want to describe the intimate details of Jacqui Smith's office, but you get the idea. I took it all in. Our escort indicated the sofa. We sat down and the sofa gave an important sigh.

'Do you ever feel like a fish out of water in these sorts of places?' Sara had asked me once. 'Like, do you ever think, what the bloody hell am I doing here?'

'Sometimes. Sometimes it feels like the whole thing's going to spin round and the Men in Black will be standing there.'

On this occasion, it wasn't Will Smith standing there, but Jacqui, the home secretary.

'Way to go, girl. First female home sec, yeah,' I said, and she laughed. 'Sorry, I'm blurting.'

Perhaps I reddened a touch, but she didn't seem to mind. In fact, she was grinning from ear to ear. People tend to react to us with either abject fear or absolute warmth. She was the latter, completely open and very warm. It might not surprise you to know that I'm very good at reading body language. It came in the same pack as my other compulsions: 'Buy hyper-vigilance get body language free.' At that moment, I could tell we had made friends with the home secretary just from the way she was standing. Open, relaxed, interested. This was the way Jacqui Smith was with Sara and me.

Then came the introductions. We have a rule that I introduce us. I say, 'Hello. I'm Shy Keenan and this is Sara.' Then I take a back seat and let them get to grips with Sara – not because Sara is especially scary, but because she has a much higher profile than I do. Plus, she has that whole Mother Teresa thing going on, and people are a little awestruck by her. So it's important they feel at ease in her presence. Generally, I tend to stand back and just let whoever we're meeting get over her and deal with her. Within two minutes of talking to her, they're completely relaxed. To be honest, even if they are a bit tense about meeting her, they completely relax in no time at all. She just has a way of putting you at your ease.

Next, the most amazing thing happened. The home secretary started singing our praises. She said some incredibly kind, nice things about us, very respectful and very, very sweet. So we had this weird moment in which all three of us were telling each other how great we thought each other was.

'You're great.'

'No, you're great.'

'No, you're greater.'

It was truly surreal to be sitting in the Home Office, three women all batting compliments around. Then we got down to business.

We talked about the whole plan. We told her all about RARE. She said that it was unlikely that the government could help financially, but they might be able to consider helping us to secure a property.

Oh. My. God. I thought. The kind of property we were looking at was going to cost – what? – a million? It had to be a big place. A place where you can do all the learning, where the team could be with units and the victims could be with the police. Plus, it would have to be safe, tranquil, peaceful.

It was going well. We talked to her about some of the cases we deal with – many of the same cases we've been telling you about. She was distraught by some of the things we had to say, intrigued and repelled by the idea of the OSC. She could see the need for RARE. It was all going very well.

Beside me, Sara was thinking the same thing. We weren't exchanging glances, not looking at one another, because that would have given our feelings away. Instead we were signing messages to each other.

This is going well.

This is definitely going well.

It's not quite sign language, obviously; it's more a kind of sign body language.

Sara explained that we understood that there probably wouldn't be any hard cash, but that help with securing the building would be great. What we had to do now, Jacqui said, was come back with a proposal and budget outline. Where and what building? What we were planning to do with the building, who we planned to hire, how much the upkeep would cost, what our long-term objectives were, who else would be funding the project and so on.

We left the Home Office floating on a magic carpet. We were filled with hope and enthusiasm. If we'd been characters in a blockbuster movie, we would have punched the air and given each other high fives and Aerosmith would have sung our theme tune.

All we needed to do now was draw up the proposal. As soon as we got back behind our respective desks, we rolled up our sleeves and went to work.

We spent three solid weeks working on that proposal. We identified a property, laid out a budget, outlined the personnel requirements, even named exactly who we planned to hire: higher-ups in the world of child protection, ex-senior police officers – we gave actual names of people who were ready to work for RARE. We listed the victim recovery team, family-liaison officers, a qualified psychologist and counsellors. We wanted to show that everyone was qualified, that these people were specialists in their field. We were able to be detailed and realistic with the budget because various contacts in the media and other interests had already told us that if we got the government behind us, they would help financially and with promotion of an in-yer-face, long-running campaign.

We talked about developing a template of care for victims. The idea was that we could draw something up and give it to the government. We would collaborate and collectively come up with a set of guidelines that would be used up and down the country. What is more, we would even help to train people to use this template. At last victims would get a fairer deal. We wanted to work with the government. We knew that we would have to work with them in order to introduce our policies: wangle, argue. We knew that we might not get everything we wanted straight away. We might at first get a team with an advocate, not the solicitor. We knew that the government had to be seen to be doing things a certain way, and we understood that they couldn't be seen to be backing some of the more campaigning elements of our work.

We were cool with all that. We knew about treading carefully. We don't go into things like a bull at a gate. We don't bang on tables. We just let the facts speak for themselves. Besides, what we were asking for was not controversial stuff. It was all about helping victims and putting children first.

Jacqui needed examples, so we put them together for her: Joe Ordinary and his wife have just found out their daughter's gone missing. The police would call us in, the Victim Trauma Impact Team. The team would help the family where they need it most. If the family needs a retreat, well, we have one. If they need a counsellor, they can meet the RARE counsellor. If they can't help, the RARE team will find somebody who can. If they need practical support, our team will be on hand to help keep their lives together as they work through the trauma. If things are going wrong as far as the services or the system is concerned, the victims and their families would have access to a victim's advocate able to act swiftly to get things back on course. The idea is that this team would be there when needed to stop the victim's lives imploding.

Having detailed our budget, given examples of how it would work, who we'd employ and so on, we forwarded the whole package of proposals to Jacqui's office. We put hard copies in the post and sent one by email. We kissed the envelope and crossed our fingers. This was our best chance at getting the government behind RARE, which made it our best chance at actually getting RARE. All we had to do now was wait.

46

After about two weeks, I started calling. It wasn't a good time. It was summer 2007 and the government was in a state of flux because Tony Blair had upped sticks and left. Gordon Brown had come in. There was nobody who could help me right now. Could I call back later? Take a ticket and wait in the queue, that kind of thing.

So I did. And we waited some more. We kept our fingers crossed, only now the enthusiastic, hopeful smiles had been replaced by a different expression: worry. When I looked at Sara on Skype, I saw my own cheek-chewing, lip-biting anxiety staring right back at me. How come they hadn't come back to us to say, 'Well done, ladies, you knocked it out of the park with that RARE proposal. Three weeks' hard work well done. Here's the building. Here's the keys'?

How come the only noise they were making was silence?

We started to wonder whether we were travelling down a dead-end road. We were swallowing hard.

Still there was no reply. The dust seemed to settle. Jacqui Smith remained home secretary after all the big changes, so we breathed a sigh of relief on that score at least. Still we waited. Still no response.

The Home Office kept coming to us for our help on other cases and we did as always and helped wherever we could. In the end, though, after several months, we gave up asking them about RARE.

A while later, we were asked by the newspapers (who had been following our RARE progress) for an update, including our meeting with the home secretary. We had to tell them that despite our earlier enthusiasm, it didn't look good.

Sara and I both felt that we'd reached an impasse. We needed money to get the RARE Retreat up and running. If we could raise the money to help victims one on one, then we ought to be able to raise it for the retreat. Money was money. We just needed to get more of it. Ultimately, though, we knew we couldn't raise enough money on our own to get the retreat started because we were already struggling to raise enough funds for our work as it was. Funding had always been a major obstacle for us. Sara and I would both look at other organisations who seemed to get by on their funding and we'd wonder why them and not us.

It had always been this way even back when we were Phoenix Survivors. We have many wealthy contacts, of course, including an airline owner, a media owner, a computer millionaire – well, billionaire, really – and one or two members of the aristocracy. These people are among the very rich and the very, very famous. We are extremely lucky to know wealthy people who trust us and believe in what we do. They are our supporters and friends, but they wouldn't remain supporters and friends for very long if all we ever did was ask them for cash.

We needed to find our money in different ways, and that's just not where our strength lies. When it comes to raising money, we are – for want of a better word – crap. We're good advocates, but what we're not good at is rattling the tin. We chewed our lips about it for a while. We looked at one another as though both trying to figure out the answer to a tricky crossword puzzle. But no. In the end, we had to admit that we're just rubbish at raising money, and there was no way we could be advocates *and* fundraisers.

We simply didn't have the money to keep going as we had been. We couldn't afford to fund the retreat and keep working on individual cases. We'd struggled for a long time to keep Phoenix Survivors going, but something had to give, something had to change. So we did some more lip-chewing. Some more staring at one another across Skype.

Do we keep on mopping up, helping victims one on one, or do we fix the dam and build the retreat? If we keep on mopping, we thought, then we'll be forever saving the poor souls who fall through the holes in the system, and we'll spend our lives working ourselves to the bone doing that, helping a few people at a time.

We're just ordinary women. We couldn't do both. If we wanted to concentrate on raising the money for RARE, then that would mean turning our back on all those cries for help that there wouldn't be time to answer. What was more important, dealing with the problems the system causes, or going after the system and stopping it causing problems in the first place?

Fighting only the biggest fights would mean big changes for us. We knew that if we were to have any hope of changing unhelpful laws, guidelines and policies, we would need to change the way we worked. It wouldn't be easy, but it soon became clear that change was our only way forward. We had to hope that if we succeeded, these changes would eventually trickle down and start making a difference to those individuals we were trying to help. It was case of having to put our resources where they could do most good. We decided we had to throw ourselves into helping the many.

Sara and I were about to make one of the hardest decisions we'd ever had to make.

After all the years of fighting to keep Phoenix Survivors going, I had to face the reality that it was time to close it down. I was devastated. We both were. The papers reported our closure and I cried a river that day.

Not for myself, I promise, but for those we knew would not get the help they needed and for all the fights we just couldn't afford to win. Sara and I spent hours talking about how we could move forward and in the end we agreed that we would always stand by certain projects but that we should change the way we worked. This would reduce the costs and allow us to keep going in some shape or form for the longest possible time.

The website went to just a holding page. Our virtual door, which had been open to victims for so long – effectively, since that day on the steps at Liverpool Crown Court – was now closed. In its place we opened the Phoenix Chief Advocates, who were me, Sara and, as always, our ever-faithful support team. We would continue to support what we call our remit cases – Sarah's Law, the Anti-Victim Prejudice and Discrimination Law, the European Child Rescue Alert, Hannah's Law, Lewis's Law, Shirley's Law and so on – but what we couldn't do was take on any new cases. When not concentrating on our remit cases, we would continue to campaign for RARE. Though where on earth the funds were going to appear from, we had no idea, given all the doors that slammed in our faces.

Then something happened that seemed to put everything else in the shade.

Sara almost died.

47

I remember thinking, Dear Fate, I've found a friend whom I love unconditionally down to my toenails. I would literally peel the skin from my bones for her and now you're going to take her from me? Don't you dare. Don't you *bloody* dare.

'I've got a banging headache, Shy,' she'd said to me the night before.

She'd suffered with migraines a lot in recent years. They lasted two or three days and caused her intense pain, made her feel sick and light-headed, the works. She managed to control them with painkillers and a sense of humour. What we do is very, very stressful. You have to expect the odd side effect. As far as she was concerned, headaches were just part of the job, like other people have pension schemes or Christmas parties.

Then one night, she had a headache unlike any other she'd experienced.

'It threw me to the floor,' she told me later. 'It literally threw me to the floor. I've never felt pain like it.'

She felt sick and hot – so hot that she went to sit outside even though it was the middle of the night. Her family were concerned, wanted to call her an ambulance, but she wouldn't let them. She's like that, our Sara, stubborn as a mule.

The next day, she got some painkillers, but the headache wouldn't go. It came in waves, some worse than others. It ebbed and flowed. She was working but not at full speed and I could tell something was up, that this headache was a bit different. Worse.

'It's killing me, Shy,' she said at last. 'I'm going to have to go and have a lie-down.'

I phoned later that night to speak to her. A friend answered and explained that she was in bed.

'Don't bother her,' I said. 'Let her rest. We'll talk later.'

But we didn't. I got a call from Sara's family to tell me she was in hospital; they'd scanned her brain and it was bleeding. It was touch and go.

As soon as I put down the phone, I burst into tears. I prayed to her guardian angels and had a screaming fit. I paced my living room, using every swearword I knew and some I was making up as I went along, cursing Fate and genetics for what was happening to her. Because, *come on*, hasn't she been through enough?

The next few hours passed by in a petrified blur. I knew what brain bleeds could do to people and I couldn't bear to think of Sara having numb areas, being unable to communicate or having huge personality changes.

Then a call came in, a sleepy-sounding Sara. She had come round and wanted me to know she was OK. I held my breath, waiting to see if she sounded the same. Had her personality been changed?

'All right, girl?' I said.

'Is that you, Shy?'

'Yeah, sweetheart, it's me.'

'How do I sound?'

How did she sound? Like Sara, only a little slower, a touch groggy. But still like Sara. She sounded like my friend. I allowed myself to feel a bit relieved. Just a bit, mind.

'You sound really good. A little drunk, maybe,' I said. 'How do you feel?'

'I don't know,' she said. 'I'm really not sure.'

'Darling,' I said, 'pick your nose and if your finger's in your eye, something's wrong.'

'Right,' she said, 'I'll give it a go. OK, my finger's definitely in my nose.'

'Then I think you'll be all right,' I said, and allowed myself almost the full dose of relief as we began laughing together.

Then she was telling me off for making her laugh.

'All right,' I said. 'Let's hear it. Tell me how come you've ended up with doctors poking around inside your head.'

She told me the story. How that night after speaking to me, the headache had kicked in so fiercely that she finally relented. The pain was so bad, the light so blinding, the nausea so great. At last, she let her family take her to the hospital. There, they eventually gave her a CAT scan. Then they moved her to another hospital and gave her another CAT scan. The following morning, she met with a surgeon, who told her they were going to operate the next day.

'And if we don't operate?' she asked.

'We're operating,' he insisted, adding, 'You're lucky – I don't normally get to have a conversation with my patients.'

'What do you mean?'

'Because the state that you're in, you should be either in a coma or have had a serious stroke. You're very lucky to be alive right now, and even more lucky to be functioning the way you are. You're having the operation.'

And that was that.

Though there were no outward signs, an artery in her brain had burst, otherwise known as an aneurysm, a bleeding brain.

And the pain. 'You know when you stand up and hit your head on a cupboard?' she explained later. 'Like that, except all the time. And the sickness was awful – just awful.'

It had been touch and go. They were expecting her to have a stroke.

'You're lucky to be alive,' she was told, innumerable times in the hospital.

'I guess I must have somebody watching over me,' she told me later, thinking of Sarah, and her mum, dad and brother, who had all died in the last few years. 'So maybe all those people, Shy,' she continued, 'are watching over me. I've got more guardian angels than anyone else. You lot only get one or two and I get loads.'

She wasn't out of the woods yet though, as I was to find when I visited her in hospital.

I found myself looking at a very pale Sara with a new, tender-looking horseshoe-shaped scar just below the hairline over her right eye. The doctors explained that she had a crucial ten days ahead of her.

For me, looking at her then, it was a moment that underlined how I had moved on as a person. I realised how much Sara meant to me. It was amazing to me that I had girls as friends, people I loved, admired and even aspired to be more like. Before, I'd never had what you might call positive female role models in my life; in fact, to be honest, I didn't really like women very much. Most of my friends were male, and all the women I did know weren't people I felt I could look up to or ever aspire to be.

Then I had met Sarah Macdonald in 2000. She was the producer on the *Newsnight* documentary that exposed Claridge and his mates. She's clever and beautiful and funny, and on top of all that she makes BAFTA-winning documentaries, real groundbreaking programmes. She, too, is unafraid to go where most angels fear to tread and has risked her own life in pursuit of the truth. As a result, she is one of the most respected in her field.

Sarah Mac and I have stayed firm friends and now work together developing documentaries and films. We are also working on my song writing and art exhibits. If it had not been for Sarah, I don't think I would have been as open to all the wonderful friendships I have since made, like the one with Shirley or the very special one I have with Sara.

Sara is so much more than a friend; there is nothing I wouldn't do for her. She comes across as very unassuming, but make no mistake, behind that fringe is an incredibly smart, intelligent woman who is taking in every word you say (even when it looks like she isn't) and quietly adding it up for herself. She learns fast and throws herself in at the deep end. She speaks her mind, which makes it easy to be her friend. Easy because you always know where you stand with her. She is so funny that she makes what

can be an unrelentingly difficult job bearable and sometimes even fun – like when we have to speak at professional conferences and I'm freaking out because there are
so many people in the room and am sweating like three
men at a coal face. She will cut through all of that for
me with a look or a few words and have me in fits of
laughter. Before I know it, I've forgotten my worries and
am getting on with the job at hand.

She has a way about her that I can't put into words. Many
people have described her as 'the calm crusader', which is
the best description I can think of. Many of the people we
advocate for get a lot out of talking to her. One distraught
mother told me that she felt like she was falling to bits and
losing her way, but that after talking with Sara for just a
while, she had managed to put things into some kind of
perspective and start caring more about herself. Sara has a
way about her that rubs off on those around her.

Not only that, but we work so well together. One of
the special elements to our friendship is our expectations
of each other. We expect each other to do well and we
compete with each other to do better. We help and
encourage each other to overcome the obstacles we face.
Every time Sara achieves a new goal, it makes me work
so much harder to catch her up, and when I succeed, she
is by my side in the same race.

Our skills complement one another, too. Sara doesn't
like making lists or writing things down; I do. I'm good
at figuring out whose door to knock on; she's good at
getting it open. I hate travelling; she doesn't mind. I don't
like being around strangers; she won't let me get away
with it.

Despite my issues trusting women, my friendships with Sarah Mac and Sara had kind of snuck up on me. That day in the hospital helped me to realise I had changed, but it also let me see when that change had started.

Sara stayed so courageous throughout the whole ordeal. I didn't need a big, scary, life-threatening health crisis to remind me of how much I care about Sara, but it worked anyway. These days, I do more to make sure she knows I care about her. She did, in the end, after some initial scary ups and downs, make a full and surprisingly speedy recovery. She had to, of course. She still had a lot of work to do.

Part Four

Rebuilding the Dam

48

In September 2008, Sara, still recovering from the tumour, made the most significant breakthrough in her campaign for Sarah's Law to date. That month, Sarah's Law was adopted on a trial basis in four areas of the country. It meant that in those areas, a person could walk into a police station armed with a name and – providing they had good cause to – check whether that person was on the Sex Offenders Register. For Sara, it was huge. It was the biggest change in the law since she had started the campaign nearly eight years earlier. She had always wanted Sarah to be remembered for protecting children and not for being murdered, and this was the first day of that hoped-for legacy.

'You cannot protect children by protecting sex offenders,' she says. It's one of her mantras. It's largely thanks to her that society is finally getting the message.

Then, in October 2008, came the Women of the Year Awards lunch at Guildhall in London. If there was one major turning point after the blow of the RARE appeal, of having to close Phoenix Survivors and of Sara's brush with death, then this was it.

It wasn't the first time it had had that effect, either. I'd been once before, back in 2005, when Sarah Mac and Sara had talked me into accepting the invitation to the annual lunch and awards ceremony. I didn't know it then, but this lunch was about to affect my life in a very special way for ever.

As you know, I'm not good with going out. It's not the place that bothers me; it's the strangers. Because I'm hyper-vigilant, I watch everybody, so the more people there are to watch, the more hyper-vigilant I become, the more I sweat. (Yes, I know, you want me sexually. Try to resist.) Neither am I a keen fan of public transport or any part of the whole dreaded travelling-into-London thing.

The first Women of the Year lunch, in 2005, was in Central London with over a hundred women attending. Can you imagine my joy, with all the women and the strangers and the travelling through London?! But Sara had talked me into going and Sarah Mac was coming with me, so there was no going back.

Far from hating it, I loved it. With Sarah Mac by my side, I made my way into the massive, ornate dining room and was immediately floored by the women there. The Women of the Year Awards celebrate women's achievements, so these were not shattered half-women who only viewed themselves through the abusive men they love (a trait I worked hard not to pick up from my own mother); these were strong, empowered, self-possessed, independently successful women who rocked the boat on their own wonderful terms.

Looking across the room, I saw Joan Armatrading and Baroness Margaret Thatcher, who both took a moment to say hello. *Bang!* Then Tina Turner. *Clunk!* She's incredibly tall, and later we argued about who was more brilliant. I won: she's more brilliant. Then I met one of my favourite funny females, Sandi Toksvig. *Thud!* I even got to kiss her. I'm sorry – did I drop a few names? I know, get me.

Seriously, though, many people that I did and did not recognise came up to say hello to me and I was taken aback by all the positive female warmth and kindness. I was in a room full of women and it was great. I felt like I had found something I didn't even know I was looking for, and before I knew it, I started to feel a bit good about being a girl. The thing is, I never had much cause to feel good about being a female; in fact, I think it's fair to say that being a girl had made me a target for so much pain that I had a bad relationship with my gender. Being a girl had made me weak, a target, a victim. Looking back, I could see that I had stayed a tomboy too long; I had always played down the girl in me; I had worked very hard to eat myself ugly and consequently I was wearing a whole other person on my bones for being so bloody stupid. Now, though, I was in a room full of amazing women who were clearly very proud to be women – women I thought I could aspire to be. I came away from that lunch with the start of a brand-new emotion: a little female pride.

Afterwards, I babbled on to Sara for hours about the day I had just had. She just sat there with her 'I told you so' grin, and she was right, she had told me so.

This, of course, was back in 2005. In 2008, I became one of the *This Morning*'s 'Wonder Women' and Sara received a Britain's Children's Champion Award from the prime minister and his wife. Sara was still recovering from the brain surgery and was just back on the Sarah's Law panel. We realised we were fast approaching what has always been a very difficult time for her: Sarah's birthday.

Sara had, in some ways, reclaimed Sarah's death day with the launch of Sarah's Law, but Sarah's birthday was still a very dark time. In the past, she had taken to her room for a week before and after, with nothing but a few bottles of liquid anaesthetic for comfort. Over the years, though, things had changed. Now, it's more like a few days either side, no drink and plenty of safe distractions. During this time, we all know to leave her be and let her lead the way on what she wants us to do to help her. That is what we were all getting ready for when out of the blue, we received the news.

A message came in from the Women of the Year team to tell us that we had been nominated for one of their major awards for our work as the Phoenix Chief Advocates and that we had won a specially arranged joint award.

I screamed. She screamed. We screamed.

Like all good friends, we both thought the other one really deserved it. I remember thinking back to how good my last experience of the awards lunch and ceremony had been, and how amazing it had been to be recognised by such a prestigious organisation.

When we received the invitations, however, a devastating blow came. The awards lunch was booked on 13 October, little Sarah's birthday.

This was a definite 'no-way' day, had been since 2000. I just didn't know what to say to Sara. We both saw the date at the same time. We looked at each other in shock. It's not that we don't talk about these difficult days – we do, but always with reverence and a respectful distance.

Here was a great big fat punch of a dilemma for Sara to consider. On the Skype screen, I could see her fighting with herself over what to do. I saw the pain she was enduring and I didn't ever want to cause her pain.

In the end, I said, 'Don't worry, sweetheart. I'll go and pick them up for both of us. Please don't worry. I will tell them about what day it is and they will understand. I can so do this.'

Then Sara looked up at the camera, directly at me, and said, 'Now tell me what you're trying *not* to say.'

Oh crap, I hate it when she does this.

'It's weird for me, Sara. I feel like I'm invading something that's yours.'

'It's OK,' she said. 'Just say it.'

'I know that the loss of Sarah is an unspeakable agony, but this day is her birthday. This was the day she was born, the day her parents cried with joy when she came into the world. I know that murdering paedophile attached himself to her death, but he has absolutely nothing whatsoever to do with her *birth*. I know it's a very sad day because of what happened, but it should also be a celebration of her birth, of your joy at her birth, of her all-too-short life. I know the organisers didn't know what day it was, but it just seems amazing to me that on the day Sarah would have become a young seventeen-year-old woman, her mother is given a Woman of the Year Award.'

'I know,' said Sara. 'It's times like this when I can almost feel her by my side, willing me to go on. This award is for her, for all the good work done in her name. I want to be there, but I just don't know if I can.'

'You tell me what you want to do and that's what we'll do.'

'Tell them we will both try to go,' she said, 'but warn them that we won't know about me until the day itself.'

I couldn't believe what I was hearing. The Women of the Year magic had already started working. Sara was actually considering going out on Sarah's birthday. If it happened, it would be a massive step forward.

As the day inched closer, we were too busy working to worry about it, and before we knew it, Sara and I were standing on the plaza of London's Guildhall, all dressed up and ready to go in. How had we got this far? By concentrating on each other. I was far too occupied with worrying about Sara to fret about traffic, strangers or any of my usual stuff; she was too busy worrying about me to think too much about what day it was.

We made our way in and met the Women of the Year team. We were chatting about the day ahead when I became aware of a fuss, a commotion, over in one corner. The event organisers seemed very upset. They looked like people who were about to fire people. They came over and pulled Sara to one side. I can read lips and body language, and I could see that they were desperately apologising to Sara.

By the time I took the few steps needed to join them, I had spotted the problem for myself. One of the team was standing there with a Woman of the Year Award in each hand and on them were inscribed the names 'Shy Keenan and *Sarah* Payne'.

They were apologising, promising to put them right, pleading for forgiveness, when Sara very calmly turned to them and said, 'Sarah did that. This is her day, her award. I'm just here to pick it up for her. It's only right that it should have her name on it.' She turned to me. 'Isn't that right, Shy?'

'I would be proud to have my name next to your daughter's, Sar,' I replied.

You have never seen six more relieved event organisers. We were all touched by Sara's grace and her very tangible connection to Sarah that day. She made me cry. I tried not to show it, but I couldn't help the old wet eyes.

I felt blessed. I had never met Sarah, but over the years her mother and I have talked about her and enjoyed some of her mum's fondest memories, and despite her daughter having one of the most recognisable faces in this country, there is still something very private about little Sarah's relationship with her family and indeed with her mum. To be included in this very private space was an honour and made me feel incredibly humble.

Then came our big moment. I had, as always, written down what I was going to say and Sara had memorised what she wanted to say. Then the amazing Helena Kennedy QC and the head of Barclays Bank came on to the stage to announce our award. I was now shaking like a leaf, mouth dry, sweating, legs like jelly. Oh my goodness, no. Legs, don't fail me now. Sara looked at me, concerned, and I smiled back, thinking, I promise you, girl, if you can make it this far, then I am definitely going to make it the rest of the way.

Our names were announced. We stood up and started to make our way to the stage. At first, I thought that those around me were standing up to allow me the space to pass – you know, wide load and all that – but by the time I had got round our table, the whole room was on its feet and clapping for us. For a second, I stopped dead in my tracks, desperately trying not to freak out. Sara turned and looked at me. Without a thought, she took my hand and walked us both to the stage.

I was so touched I was crying inside by the time I got to the podium. Despite my best efforts, the first part of my thank-you speech was at that high, shaky, I'm-trying-not-to-cry-out-loud pitch, spoken at about 90 miles per hour. Sara was much calmer and again brought tears to my eyes. Before we knew it, we were off the stage and smiling our heads off in the green room. We then met some of the ladies at the lunch and made many new friends. The Women of the Year lunch had indeed worked its magic on us both.

We came away from that day in very high spirits. We had both taken some big steps forward and we could feel it. And the best thing? Having a good friend to share it with. It doesn't get much better than that, does it?

We certainly didn't set out to do any networking that day – personally, my priority was Sara – but by the end of the afternoon, we'd collected countless offers of support and backing. Real, tangible support, too. If our heads had bowed a fraction on the closure of Phoenix Survivors, if our shoulders had drooped slightly as we negotiated the gloom of that time, then now we were holding our heads high again. People believed in us. They wanted to listen to what we had to say. We left that lunch as the proud bearers of Women of the Year Awards, but also with high hopes for the future.

Epilogue

After the Women of the Year Awards, as we were having our picture taken, the current attorney general, Baroness Scotland, walked up, threw her arms around us and said, 'These are my girls.' Sara and I looked at each other and smiled. Of course, we both admire and respect the attorney general, but this touched us deeply, and Sara knew it would touch me more than the baroness might have realised.

For me personally, when it came to society, its establishments and systems, I had always felt like an outsider. I regarded myself as excluded, unwanted crack chaff, considered most likely to waste my life. Yet here I was, after all these years, after everything, one of the attorney general's 'girls'.

As usual, as I stood there being photographed, with that great big flash going off in my face, I tried hard to block out the unwelcome thoughts that try to invade and undermine such wonderful moments. I couldn't help my mind going back to my childhood, but this time it felt very different. Yes, I was thinking about how helpless and voiceless I used to be. Yes, I remembered how difficult it had been to get the judicial establishment to hear me, let alone protect me. Yes, I remembered how alone and frightened I used to feel . . . but something fundamental had changed. I realised that I 'used' to feel voiceless; I 'used' to feel invisible and alone; I 'used' to feel a lot of things that I just don't feel so much anymore. As I stood there, feeling loved, supported, included and heard, an indescribable lifelong ache just lifted.

There was very little that could top the Women of the Year lunch. Sara and I had been honoured by all of those who had reached out to us in our roles as the Phoenix Chief Advocates and allowed us close enough to try and help them. We have the most amazing supporters you could ever hope for, and we get to work with the very best. We have certainly learned a lot.

RARE was and is still very much our priority. We knew we needed to make sure the victim's needs are put first across the system, but without government support or funding, we realised we couldn't have RARE just yet. What we could do, however, was continue to promote the RARE philosophy to anyone who would listen and hope that one day soon our voices would reach the right ears. Fingers crossed, as always.

As 2008 drew to a close, Sara and I found ourselves talking more and more about the future. There were many incredible people out there doing their bit in this fight. We both felt that despite the problems we faced, society had taken huge steps and changed for the better. The trials of Sarah's Law were proof of that, as was our reception at the Women of the Year Awards and the offers of support.

The vast majority of the society we live in is made up of good, fair, decent human beings who instinctively protect children. We have known all along that most people would be horrified if they knew that the system was hurting and not helping victims in their name. Now, at long last, society was finally seeing what was happening and wanted change as much as we did.

We have talked about some of the cases we have worked alongside, and although they are sadly just the tip of the iceberg, there is real hope in the midst of all this horror. While it is true that we have been where most angels would fear to tread and seen the worst that some people can do (and will do), we have also seen the very wonderful things that people can achieve. We have witnessed incredible, inspirational human courage, met many brave child protectors who go above and beyond the call of duty, watched the system working and working well. We have seen supported victims rebuilding a good life from the wreckage left by a paedophile's crimes. We've also seen our communities working together with the authorities to stand up to the sex-offender community and win.

Whether we are the victim or the family of victims, the fact is that we need society to include us, embrace us and help us to rise from the ashes. In turn, we need to help our society. One of the first things victims have to do is unlearn any bad lessons that paedophiles have tried to teach them. We also need to help our society unlearn all that rubbish. We need to show them our amazing 83 per cent and help our society wherever we can to develop the best possible child protection.

Maybe it's time we changed how we work with society, its establishments and systems. Maybe it's time to take our fingers out of the dam and start rebuilding the dam altogether. But how? How do we get close enough to the system so that when we talk, it listens?

As we continued searching for answers to these questions, they were answered for us in the form of two wonderful New Year's gifts. For years and years we've been talking about how the unspeakable horror of being a paedophile victim is compounded by the horror of what happens next. We've been trying to tell people that as a victim, your needs are ignored and your pain goes untreated. We've tried to explain how most people can't even hear the victim's voice over the army of voices reminding them of the offender's human rights. Often it's felt like we've been talking to a closed door, a brick wall. Now, all of that was about to change again as Sara was honoured by the Queen of England with an MBE and a few days later accepted a position at the Ministry of Justice as their first ever Victims' Champion.

At last, that door has finally opened and Sara has walked through. Now anything is possible. Now we have a voice where it really matters – a Phoenix voice.

As for the future, well, let's just say that there is always work to be done, and we will always be there to do it. But one thing is certain: come what may, we will continue to walk where most angels fear to tread.

If you are reading this within the UK and feel you need to talk to someone, please do try www.napac.org.uk or call them on 0800 085 3330. Throughout our years as victims' advocates, we've seen what kind of help works for victims and what doesn't. The National Association for People Abused in Childhood or NAPAC was set up twelve years ago and run by a true Phoenix - the amazing Peter Saunders. He runs a free support and information telephone service and has spent years helping people abused in childhood to cope with the often lifelong and sometimes devastating consequences.

Many people have told us that they would not be alive today if it were not for NAPAC. One lady told us her particular story of when she tried to get help through the 'system' and was granted six 40 minute appointments on the last Wednesday of every month, miles away from where she lived. She said her biggest problems were getting to the appointments and making sure she was ready to force out her issues on time. For the most part, she just needed someone to listen 'when she was ready to talk', and luckily NAPAC was there for her when she needed them - for as long as she needed them - which made all the difference to her recovery.

We were so impressed by the things people were saying about NAPAC that we joined their eminent list of patrons. NAPAC has just developed a template of victim care which they plan to roll out across the whole of the UK, training and accrediting support workers across the country. All they need now, yes, you've guessed it, is government funding. And, because of the data protection and victim anonymity laws that govern all such work in this field, it has to be government funding. So whilst we will always chase our own RARE dreams, we always say to those who ask us that if you want to make a donation to a registered charity that really helps victims, then please, send it to NAPAC.